SLIPCOVERS & BEDSPREADS

Slipcovers and bedspreads . . .
a natural combination for a complete
bedroom setting.

By the Editors of Sunset Books and Sunset Magazine

Lane Publishing Co., Menlo Park, California

Informal print slipcovers and mixed throw pillows complement rich rust carpet. Design: Harriet Raymond.

STAFF EDITORS:
Christine Barnes
Maureen Williams Zimmerman
Diane Petrica Tapscott

SPECIAL CONSULTANTS:
Michael Scofield
Art Bonner
Linda J. Selden

DESIGN:
Mike Valdez

PHOTOGRAPHY:
Stephen W. Marley

ILLUSTRATIONS:
Susan Jaekel
Mike Valdez

Sunset Books
Editor, David E. Clark
Managing Editor, Elizabeth L. Hogan

Fifth printing August 1987

From idea to reality...

When the season—or your mood—changes, think about sewing slipcovers to dress up and protect your furniture. Or if your bedroom needs waking up, turn yards of fabric into a new bedspread that will brighten the entire room. This book opens with a gallery of decorating ideas in color, then offers step-by-step instructions and illustrations for making your own slipcovers and bedspreads.

The projects that follow require basic sewing skills, as well as time and patience, but they are not difficult and the rewards are great.

It takes the time and cooperation of many people to put together a book like this. In addition to the designers whose names appear in the photo captions, we wish to thank the following persons and places for their help: Pat Adams, Ambert's Furniture, Art Bonner Slip Covers, Ida Brown, Casa Marin, Joanne and Ronald Dingwall, Downtown Singer Sewing Center, Ethan Allen American Traditional Interiors, Andrea Fanslow, Finlay's Slipcovers, Gene Forrest, The Great Cover Up, Sharon Groeneveld, Mitzi Hall, Kaufman's Fabric Land, Mollie Kellner, Eileen and Bob Korjenek, Cheryl Madsen, Dorothy McKown, Madge McPherson, New York Fabrics, Mary Sue Odegard, Paula Paul, Lydia Pietrosilli, Paul Schagen Fabrics, Marge Scott, Peg Stanfield, Paula Traherne, Marie White, and C.T. Wilkins. In particular, we wish to thank Sharon Multhauf and Sudha Irwin for their editorial contributions, which were so valuable to the content of this book.

CONTENTS

Large pillows echo the simple but elegant machine-quilted comforter. Design: Michael Taylor.

SLIPCOVERS & BEDSPREADS
...decorating ideas

A place to start, this section of the book is meant to inspire you as you're pondering what kind of slipcover or bedspread you want. It will be your guide as you try to narrow the fabric possibilities and visualize how the finished project might look in your home.

The examples shown here are not to be taken too literally—use them as departure points for your own imagination. Specific fabric designs come and go, but you'll be able to see how a general type of fabric will look. The exact piece of furniture you want to cover may not be duplicated here, but you're almost certain to see pieces that are similar. The rooms won't be the same as yours, but you'll be able to see how an effect was achieved. The ideas shown, plus your own creativity, will put you well on your way to a slipcover or bedspread that's right for your home.

Softening details—the gathered corners of skirts, the throw pillows with ruffled edges—make these crisp, striped slipcovers special. Made of sheets, they were economical because of extra fabric width. Design: Kate O'Dea Pacoe.

A puffy comforter may not tuck neatly under pillows, but you can add the finishing touch of pillow shams like these. Green bias binding trims pillow sham ruffles; machine quilting ripples across comforter. Design: René Vergez.

SLIPCOVERS DRESS UP THESE ROOMS

Grouping of slipcovered pieces combines two garden-fresh fabrics for a complementary effect. Throw pillows relate white sofa to green zebra-striped chairs. Extra-thick welt accents chairs' seams. Design: Judith Joyce.

Peppy tomato background of floral print stands out vividly against pale walls and carpeting. Welted seams and gathered skirts finish slipcovers for sofa, chairs, and ottoman. Design: Judith Joyce.

Reliable way to mix fabrics:
choose a solid to accent a print as
the white sofas in this quartet accent
the chairs. Straight lines of furniture
are emphasized by welt, tailored
skirts. Design: Harriet Raymond.

SOFAS

Take a straightforward sofa, add a special fabric

Medley of prints on sofa, wallpaper, and throw pillows creates cheerful, casual look. The same basic colors tie varied prints together. Design: Benita McConnell.

Two white sofas…
two different effects

Outlined with cocoa-colored welt, white linen-look sofa presents trim, tailored appearance. Contrast welt also accents boxed cushions on back and deck, as well as skirt.

Soft design of this white slipcover includes knife-edge single seat cushion and ample, squishy back cushions. Lacking the usual skirt, the sofa looks all the more streamlined.

Side-by-side sofas wear fabric with a freeform motif, requiring less precision in centering and matching than most bold prints do. Unmatched stripes run over deck cushions, fronts of sofas, and skirts. The slightly mismatched pattern combines with weltless seams to exaggerate the undulating look of the fabric. Design: Elva Powell.

Sofas slipcovered for a lavish look

Turning a corner, this L-shaped sofa provides plenty of seating. Dark blue to pale brown print harmonizes with room. Large motif is centered on each cushion and on outside arms.

LOVE SEATS

Plain or printed, slipcovers can be striking

Like waves breaking, pattern flows over love seat. This pattern didn't have to be matched. Welt on inside back lines up with the three loose deck cushions. Design: Phyllis Dunstan.

From Sri Lanka, rust and white batik lends a sprightly note of distinction to love seat and chair cushion. The exotic cotton accents the deep red of the rug and Parsons table. Design: René Vergez.

Contrast welt defines graceful contours of wing love seat, while the row of contrasting pillows stands out sharply against pale slipcover fabric. Design: Marge Matthews.

...LOVE SEATS

Double the impact with slipcovers in matching pairs

Diagonal stripes in bright colors enliven their quiet, neutral-toned surroundings. Though they run rhythmically at the same angle, the stripes are not perfectly matched. Groups of petite yellow throw pillows pick up the cheeriest color in the slipcovers, their floral print providing a pleasing contrast to the stripes.

Cool white duck slipcovers, tunnel quilted for extra luxury, usher in the lazy days of summer. The two comfortable love seats have welted seams, knife-edge cushions.

Chocolate and white motif perks up this pair of love seats. Plump, knife-edge back cushions and skirtless design enhance gently curving lines of furniture.

...LOVE SEATS

Distinctive fabrics turn into special slipcovers

Bold, Imari-look print was artfully arranged to make the dark stripes wrap this small love seat like wide ribbon. Skirtless slipcover style shows off the intricate detail of the fabric pattern.

Matching fabric-covered walls and love seat invite you to this cozy corner. Not part of the print, contrasting borders were stitched separately to skirt strip and fronts of pillows before these pieces were seamed. Design: Corinne Wiley.

CHAIRS

Patterns—centered or matched—create one-of-a-kind slipcovers

Wide bands of pattern line up vertically on this handsome and comfortable chair. While the fabric is unusual, with its rich, Oriental-looking details, the slipcover style is straightforward: welted seams and a simple, tailored skirt.

Pair of armchairs with large white-on-brown motif combines with pink lamp, footstool, and tablecloth to make a most inviting conversation corner. Dramatic motif is centered on the slipcovers' backs, on T-shaped deck cushions, and on fronts and skirts. Design: Esther H. Reilly.

Fresh floral slipcovers dress up cozy chairs

A dense thicket of soft greens and blues in this slipcover with tailored skirt conveys a peaceful mood. Two welted seams divide the inside back of this barrelback chair from the inside arms. Design: Esther H. Reilly.

Dainty, twining flowers, pink and lavender on a white background, give these chairs a delicate look. Softly gathered skirts emphasize romantic, feminine appeal. Design: Christine Johnson.

Update the familiar wing chair with a striped, printed, or solid slipcover

Licorice ticking stripes give a contemporary, casual air to the usually more formal wing chair. Perfect matching of stripes was essential to the neat, tailored look.

Traditional wing chair takes to slipcovering in an updated chintz. Skirtless bottom reveals dark and elegant Queen Anne legs.

Solid-color and severe, this slipcover draws attention to the striking design of the chair: a pattern would have distracted attention from its elegant lines. Trim around skirtless edge draws the eye to fanciful swirls of wood. Shirred boxing makes cushion look soft and inviting, and contrasts with chair's high back and extended wings. Design: Harriet Raymond.

TIED-ON SLIPCOVERS
Ties give slipcovers a secure fit and casual look

Faced with a print, decorative bands tie skirted cushions to bamboo chairs. Each crisp skirt covers its cushion along front and sides, but back seams are left open to slip over backs of chairs.

Outlined by quilting, fish appear to leap in the batik cushion covers on this rattan sofa. Cushions have welted knife edges; ties attach those at the back to sofa. Design: Benita McConnell.

DAY BEDS

Cushions and bolsters compose these day beds

Antique day bed frame of mellow-toned wood receives the luxury of cushions covered in raw silk. Three cushion styles combine effectively here: the deck cushion has a knife edge hidden inside the frame; shirred boxing accents the back cushions; throw pillows feature soft flanges. Design: Harriet Raymond.

Gray and beige plaid streamlines upholstered frame, as well as bolsters and mattress cover. Broad stripes on carpeting continue the gray and beige theme through the room. What you see in the corner of the day bed is not a plump pussycat but a cushion covered in fake fur. Design: Gary Bond.

Railroading—running the chevrons horizontally—on the deck cushion, in contrast to the side cushions, gives this day bed a cozier, more compact look. Had all the fabric been railroaded, the angled sides would have been less clearly defined. Bargello print contrasts brightly with dark wicker frame. Design: René Vergez.

...DAY BEDS

Begin a color scheme with the day bed cover

Delicate mauve brightens day beds, relating them to carpet. Textural shifts from walls to spreads to floor covering add interest. Attached tailored skirts, seamed at bed edges, and round bolsters finish spreads; throw pillows provide accents. Design: Esther H. Reilly.

A chorus of greens, including five different fabrics, harmonizes beautifully with pin-striped wallpaper, pastel draperies, and solid-color rug. Head and foot boards are upholstered; tailored, custom-quilted day bed cover has welted seams. Design: William Houston.

Gathered skirts soften day beds

Fabric continues from day bed cover, its separate skirt, day bed frame, cushions, and draperies to merge with matching wallpaper for a lavishly patterned look. Orange wall repeats brightest of fabric's colors. Design: Angie May-Lin Sheldon.

Border-print skirt complements as it contrasts with blue and white spread and throw pillows, but it perfectly repeats the minute pattern of the wallpaper. The carpeting continues the tranquil shade of blue. Design: Christy Neidig/Vintage Properties.

BEDSPREADS

Bedspreads can be crisp and perky, or quilted and plush

Green plaid peeks through inverted corner pleats on the skirt of this white duck spread. More plaid appears as contrasting welt and ruffled pillow sham. Design: Christy Neidig/Vintage Properties.

Open corners of quilted, tucked-in spread fit neatly around bedposts. Handpainted pillows make distinctive accents. Design: Avis State.

The floor-length throw—a basic theme with endless variations

Four-poster bed requires a spread with open corners. Outline quilting defines blue and burgundy print; ruffled pillow shams are made of same fabric but are not quilted. Carpet, chair, and lamp all repeat the rich blue in the fabric print. Design: Christy Neidig/Vintage Properties.

Corduroy patchwork of rich colors makes attractively textured throw. Quilting defines and poufs each wide-wale square.

Thick rolled edge adds polish to this outline-quilted throw. Handsome coordinated headboard upholstery has distinctive shirred edge. Room evokes a Far Eastern mood with its Indonesian batiks, Japanese prints, Chinese lamps, Philippine rattan end tables, and Dhurrie rug from India. Design: Avis State.

...BEDSPREADS

Coverlet-length throws team up with skirts underneath

Red-patterned binding, separate skirt, and pillow shams make bold accents against a white piqué coverlet. Lamp shades, draperies, and throw pillows add more coordinated detail to the collage of prints. Design: Benita McConnell.

Wide eyelet trim edges a lined white eyelet throw. Square corners drape gracefully to floor over unpressed box pleats of separate skirt. The lacy feeling continues in trim on folded blanket cover. A potpourri of pillow shams against the distinctive upholstered headboard completes the arrangement.

Skirts—to match or not to match?

The bright print that splashes from tablecloth to spread to draperies looks softer than it would without the influence of the gathered wheat-colored skirt on the bed. The quilted coverlet-length spread has a matching pillow sham with a ruffled edge.

Gathered skirt repeats the fabric used for comforter—but does not repeat its quilting. Wide band of solid blue defines boundary of comforter, appears again as ruffled edges of pillow shams. Wallpaper reflects quietest of fabric's "patchwork" prints; table skirt enlarges on blue and white theme.

...BEDSPREADS
Tied quilts give a custom effect with minimal effort

Reversible comforter shows off companion prints, repeated in many other details—the separate skirt, pillow shams, table cover, shades, and chair cushion. White ties in comforter add yet another pattern to predominantly blue print. Design: Marianne Nicholson and Corinne Wiley.

Two twin-size sheets,
sandwiching batting and tied with
yarn, make up each of these puffy
bedspreads. Contrasting binding
makes a distinct border between
each comforter and its separate
gathered skirt.

Dainty eyelet ruffle edges yarn-tied
baby quilt. Matching the serene pattern of the quilt are cradle sheet and
pillow sham, plus fabric-covered
panel. Design: Angie May-Lin
Sheldon.

Floral border print brightens the whole room—featured in gathered skirt, wallpaper, pillows, and window treatment. Honey-colored spread lends a quieter note; coverlet-length, it has decorative quilting pattern and thick scalloped edge. Design: Linnea H. Alm.

Coordinated bedspreads, skirts, and wallpaper tie a room together

Crosshatching of green stripes blends softly box-pleated skirt with wallpaper. Spread features large floral bouquets overlaying the green cross-hatching and is finished with a thick scalloped edge. Design: Glenna Cook.

Beaded eyelet trim dresses up the white gathered skirt and matching pillow shams. Ribbon, laced through the eyelet, repeats the serene peach color of the tunnel-quilted spread. Design: Christy Neidig/ Vintage Properties.

For a feminine touch, pastel bedspreads with gathered skirts

Lavish use of striped and floral fabric sets the sunny mood in this room. The coverlet-length spread either tucks in to show the full length of the gathered skirt, or overlaps the skirt by a few inches. Quilting picks out the stripes on both coverlet and pillow shams. Design: Virginia Darcé.

SLIPCOVERS

Step by step—from choosing a fabric to putting on the finished cover

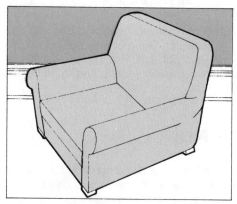

You'll soon learn how to slipcover this chair and other furniture pieces.

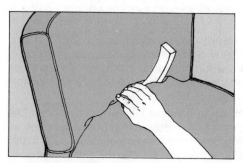

Foam wedges keep slipcovers snug.

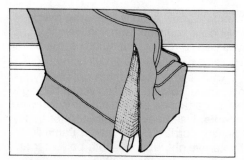

Unzip, peel off, and dry-clean—your slipcover's as good as new.

How long have you looked at the faded brocade covering on the *chaise longue* in the bedroom? Or fretted about the stains on the armchair in the den? Or wished you could perk up your living room sofa with a light-colored chintz for summer?

You could buy new furniture, have the old reupholstered, have slipcovers made, or make the slipcovers yourself. Assuming that the furniture is in fairly good condition—that it's structurally sound—keeping the furniture and changing the fabric covering may be the most economical solution. In deciding between new upholstery and slipcovers, consider the following points.

Slipcovers give your furniture a new lease on life, yet take half as long to do as a complete reupholstering job, and usually cost less.

Fully upholstered armchair

Wing chair

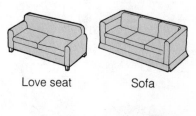

Love seat   Sofa

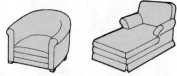

Barrelback chair   Chaise longue

By using a few thumb tacks or staples or strips of nylon self-gripping fastener at the base of your chair or sofa, and wedging rolls of paper or plastic foam into fabric tuck-ins, you can keep most slipcovers as snug and immobile as upholstery.

Slipcovers sometimes simplify the lines of a piece of furniture, to make construction easier and removal for cleaning less time-consuming. It is possible to duplicate all the upholstery seams, but you will have to modify the standard blocking-out and pin-fitting techniques given in this book, and use more tacks or pins for attachment.

Should a pet claw part of your slipcover to shreds, it's not the end of the world. Just rip out the seams of the damaged section, replace the material with new fabric, repin, and resew. Such a repair consumes a fraction of the time needed to make a similar repair on an upholstered piece. It's worth your while to buy extra fabric to keep on hand for this purpose.

Best of all, when a slipcover is soiled, you simply unzip it and send it to be dry-cleaned. Slipcovers made from bedsheets or other fabric guaranteed to be preshrunk and machine washable may even be run through a washer.

On the negative side, it's true that slipcovers sewn on a home machine often require lighter-weight fabrics than upholstery, which means they'll wear out faster with hard use. Nevertheless, if your furniture is torn or permanently soiled, or if you simply want a change, slipcovers can be the ideal answer.

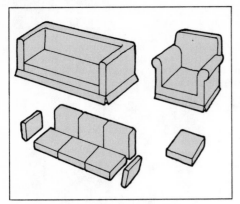

A sofa may require three times as much fabric as a chair.

Do Your Own Work?

Once you've decided on slipcovers rather than new upholstery, you still must make the choice between doing the work yourself and hiring a professional. Even if you decide to hire a professional, an understanding of the slipcover-making process will enable you to work with him or her more effectively.

A professional can do the job faster than you and will correct any mistakes at no charge. A pro has plenty of work space (you may not) and knows how to handle offbeat kinds of furniture and unforeseen problems.

On the other hand, a professional may not attend to the minute details as you would, and in some areas it is difficult to find slipcover makers. Certainly a professional will cost you more. And let's face it: there's a special thrill not only in learning a skill but in being able to say, "I did that job myself."

Once you have your tools and fabric ready, you may find that you can create a standard slipcover over a weekend. The methods outlined in this book eliminate traditional paper or muslin patterns. Pins replace traditional basting. And in most cases you need not reverse fabric and repin before stitching.

What's Easy, What's Not

Keep in mind some generalities when you are deciding what furniture to slipcover, and with what fabric. First, the larger the surface to be covered, the more work for you and the more fabric you'll have to buy. A standard 72-inch sofa with three loose deck (seat) cushions, three loose back cushions, and two arm pillows can take three times as much fabric as a single-cushioned upholstered armchair. Then there's the matter of matching patterns—trying to match up pieces of fabric printed or woven with scenes, flowers, stripes, plaids, or other patterns requires more fabric and a lot more patience than using plain colors or certain small patterns that require no matching.

Look at the number of upholstered curves your piece of furniture has. The more curves, the more cutting and pin-fitting you'll have to do in order to get a snug fit. Look, too, at the furniture's cushions. They'll be much easier to cover if you can remove them from your sofa or chair. Removable rectangular cushions are the easiest of all to cover.

Don't plan to slipcover furniture upholstered in vinyl or leather (the surfaces are too slippery), or open-arm furniture with partially upholstered arms. The difficulty of slipcovering open-arm furniture places it outside this book's scope. Furniture with lots of visible wood is also difficult to slipcover.

Tools You'll Need

The most important piece of equipment you'll need is a **sewing machine.** Any portable or cabinet model will do if you work with lightweight fabric. The more flat space with which you can surround your machine, the better.

For most slipcover fabrics, including bedsheets, you will want a #16 or #90 **needle** for your machine. If you need to patch torn upholstery first (see page 52), you'll also want fabric glue. To whipstitch polyester batting to channels or crevices on channeled or attached pillowback furniture, you'll need a curved **upholsterer's needle.** Use heavy-duty thread for heavy-duty fabrics such as sailcloth, denim, corduroy, and cotton damask; all-purpose thread works fine for lighter-weight fabrics—both polyester and cotton-wrapped polyester thread are stronger than cotton.

The **zipper foot** that comes with most sewing machines aids in installing zippers (see page 94) and welt (see page 83).

The more curves your furniture has, the more work for you. Stay clear of open-arm chairs.

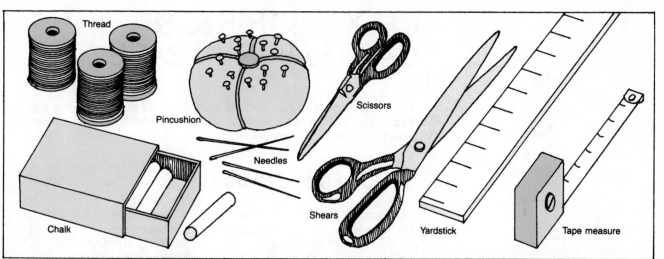

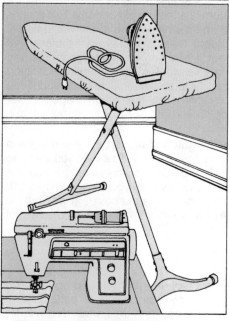

The sewing machine is basic. Use an iron to press a few seams open and to remove wrinkles.

An **iron and ironing board** are necessary for pressing a few seams open and for removing wrinkles once your cover is sewn. It's wise to use a sample of your fabric to experiment, determining the correct degree of heat, whether or not to use steam or spray (they may spot some fabrics), whether to press on the right or wrong side, and whether to use a **press cloth** to keep the fabric from becoming shiny.

It's important to own a sharp pair of bent-shank, fabric-cutting **shears** with blades at least 5 inches long. The longer the blades, the fewer cuts you have to make and the easier you'll find the task of cutting. These shears are available at fabric and hardware stores, and upholstery supply shops.

If you don't want to invest in upholsterer's shears, you can find lighter-weight, less expensive varieties at fabric shops. But keep in mind that quality steel holds its edge longer, and sharp blades cut faster through fabric folds when you're blocking out fabric. Whatever shears you buy, make sure that the handle is large enough for you to slip three fingers easily in and out. You may also want a pair of **small scissors** for clipping threads.

You'll need **pins,** of course—a box of 200 suffices for an upholstered armchair or a sofa. Flat-headed pins, called dressmaking pins, allow you to outline curved seamlines precisely. Nickel-plated brass, 1 1/16-inch flat-headed pins are ideal. Also buy sturdier **T-shaped pins** for anchor pinning fabric to the furniture.

Other slipcover tools include **chalk,** a 12-inch **ruler,** and a **yardstick.** You need these to draw the guidelines necessary for cutting out cushion boxing (see page 80) and welt strips (see page 83). Blackboard chalk makes bolder marks and is easier to brush out than tailor's chalk. Test your yardstick for straightness by setting it on edge on a tabletop.

You will also need a **tape measure** for estimating fabric needed.

How Best to Use This Book

No matter what type of upholstered furniture you want to slipcover—an arm, wing, or barrelback chair, an ottoman, sofabed, love seat, or sofa—this book shows you how to do it using the simplest techniques possible. You'll note that many of the drawings in the how-to-do-it chapters portray a fully upholstered armchair. That's because the techniques that work for such an armchair usually work for other kinds of furniture as well. When additional techniques are needed to get the job done, text and drawings explain them.

If you've never made a slipcover, you may want to practice with inexpensive bedsheets or bolt muslin first. But by following the instructions in this book and giving yourself plenty of time, you'll find that your chances are good for producing quality work on your first try.

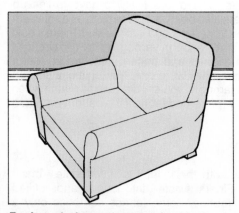

Basic techniques that work for this chair work for most other pieces.

CHOOSING FABRIC & CALCULATING YARDAGE

A dizzying variety of fabrics lend themselves to slipcovers. This section helps you select the best fabric for the job you want to do, then shows you how to determine the amount you'll need.

Which Fabric to Buy?

With today's proliferation of fabric blends, prints, and weaves, choosing the best fabric for your slipcover may at first seem impossible. Don't despair; you'll find the decision to be far simpler than you thought. The trick is to consider not the slipcover itself but the whole room.

What you mainly want for your room is a feeling of harmony. This means that your slipcover's colors should complement those of the walls, floors, draperies, and other furnishings already there. You may want professional guidance in creating the right effect. Many home furnishings stores and fabric shops offer customers the free services of their interior decorating staff. You can also find a designer through personal recommendations (probably the best method) or by checking the Yellow Pages under "Interior Decorators and Designers"; members of ASID have met various professional requirements.

It's wise to take home a good-size swatch of fabric before you make a final decision—if necessary, buy a half-yard or so. This way you can see how it goes with other fabrics and colors in the room, what effect the room's light has on the fabric, and generally how you'll like living with it. You can also make sure that the patterns on the old covering won't show through—a potential problem if the new fabric is lightweight and has lots of light-colored background.

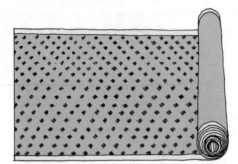

The smaller the pattern, the simpler the slipcover is to make.

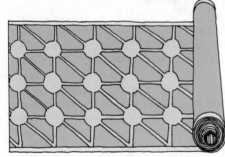

Large repeat patterns require careful matching.

Patterns or solids?

Faced with a seemingly infinite array of fabrics, you'll probably find yourself mentally classifying them as either solid colors or patterns. The decor with which your slipcover must blend may make the decision for you. But if you have a choice, consider that solid colors simplify cutting and fitting, because no matching is required. But they also show dirt more readily than do patterns.

You may decide that a pattern will give your piece of furniture just the flair it needs, but in choosing a pattern you'll probably want to consider the ease of assembling it into a slipcover. Fabrics with small, all-over patterns are the easiest to piece together—you're less likely to have to line up designs. (Small, all-over patterns are also best on a piece such as a sofabed, where two zippers extend over the front deck and into the skirt.) Here's how to know in advance: In the store, unroll enough yardage to lay two sections of fabric side by side, selvages aligned and pattern matched so that it continues across the two widths as if they were one. Now shift one section slightly—if the pattern fluctuates jarringly, you should plan to match when you make your slipcover. Don't buy patterned fabric if the pattern is printed severely off-grain.

ABCs of fabric

That both fiber and fabric begin with the letter f is unfortunate—many people confuse the two words. Fibers, twisted into long strands called yarns, are what get woven into fabrics. Some fabrics comprise only a single fiber type; others are blends of two or more fibers. Thus "cotton" refers to the fiber. "Velvet," on the other hand, does not. Like chintz, duck, and other terms you'll meet later, velvet is a type of fabric only. It can be woven from the fibers of cotton, nylon, polyester—in fact, many fibers.

Where to buy. Home furnishings stores sometimes sell fabrics, but possibly your best bet is to look in the Yellow Pages under "Fabric Shops." These outlets sell textiles in great variety, as well as supplies with which to fashion them into finished goods.

Sometimes professional upholsterers sell bolt fabrics suitable for slipcovers. They keep a supply of sample books with swatches that range from 6-inch to 18-inch squares.

Probably the best sources of distinctive bolt fabrics are interior decorators and designers. These specialists have access to high-quality fabrics you can't find elsewhere, and they will bring samples to your home. Theirs is a service, of course, for which you must expect to pay.

Department stores are usually the best source for bedsheets. Sometimes these stores devote a separate department to bolt fabrics as well.

Questions to ask yourself. When shopping for fabrics for slipcovers, you'll want answers to these questions:

1. Will the fabric wear well? Long wear depends more on a weave's tightness—the number of threads per square inch—than on the type of weave. The tighter the weave, the less the fabric stretches. You can test tightness by trying to stretch the fabric as shown (not on the bias). If you remain uncertain, try to look through the fabric—the less light you see, the denser the fabric and the tighter the weave.

2. Will my sewing machine stitch through four layers of fabric (necessary for attaching welt—see page 83)? Will it sew through nine layers (necessary for adding optional self-lined skirt)? With many thicknesses, you may have to turn the machine wheel by hand. When in doubt, buy ¼ yard of the fabric and test it on your machine.

3. Does the pattern show through the fabric's wrong side? If so, you'll find pin-fitting much easier.

4. Are the colors likely to fade? The words "Vat Dyed" or "Vat Colors" imprinted along the selvage of a fabric mean the dyes won't dissolve in water. All dyes fade somewhat; vat-dyed fabrics resist fading best. Whether vat-dyed or not, dark fabrics will show more fading, and show it sooner, than light ones.

5. Does the fabric stretch? All fabric stretches to some degree, especially on the bias. But the more it stretches, the more likely it is to lose its shape as a slipcover.

6. How often must I clean the fabric? The lighter the color and the plainer the fabric, of course, the more readily you'll see grime. Synthetic fibers repel soiling better than natural fibers, but natural fibers clean better once soiled. Safest are those fabrics imprinted with the words "soil-resistant" or the equivalent.

7. How much will the fabric shrink? Natural fibers shrink more than synthetics. Most cotton denim shrinks 6 percent. Even so-called "preshrunk" fabric shrinks 1 to 2 percent. Whether or not you see "preshrunk" or "Sanforized" imprinted on the fabric's edge, it's a good idea to ask a dry cleaner to steam-shrink the fabric before you cut (steam-shrinking instead of washing keeps fabric finishes and most colors intact); in the case of bedsheets, wash and dry them at the temperatures you will use later. That way, when you clean the finished cover, shrinkage will be no problem.

Taking the plunge. Whether you purchase your bolt fabric from a fabric shop, home furnishings or department store, upholsterer, or independent interior decorator, be sure to examine all the material carefully, checking for correct pattern, color, and fabric width, and for any flaws and misweaves. Returns or trades are rarely allowed once you begin to cut.

It's always wise to purchase more fabric than you expect to need—½ yard for a chair, 1 yard for a larger piece. You may not need it, but usually only the most experienced slipcover makers can determine fabric needs

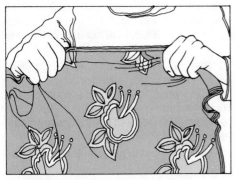

Fabric with a tight weave is best because it stretches less.

Fabrics that stretch a great deal on the bias should be avoided.

"Vat Colors" or "Vat Dyed" means fabric is colorfast.

with absolute precision, and the security of having a little leeway is well worth the extra cost, since fabric designs, like clothing styles, disappear fast. If you make a cutting mistake, or decide later you want arm protectors, chances are your fabric will no longer be available. This holds true both for bolt fabrics and bedsheets.

When buying a bolt fabric, buy all of it off the same bolt. The same design's coloring may vary from bolt to bolt if the fabric was dyed at different times or in different vats.

The most popular slipcover fabrics

Cotton constitutes the base for most of the fabrics suitable for slipcovers. That's because cotton is long-lasting and inexpensive, it hugs the furniture well without tacks, and it is easily cleaned and pressed. Most cotton-based slipcover fabrics are 100 percent cotton. Others combine cotton with polyester (such as bedsheets), and cotton with linen. The polyester gives a fabric wrinkle and soil resistance; the linen gives it crispness.

Besides cotton, other natural fibers include flax (from which linen is made), silk, and wool. They all have disadvantages—expect to deal with wrinkles if you buy 100 percent linen; wool can feel scratchy on bare skin, and because it stretches, you may find wool difficult to pin-fit; silk adds elegance but is slippery and expensive, and it tends to curl while you work with it.

Two factors keep 100 percent synthetics—the acetates, acrylics, nylons, olefins, polyesters, and rayons—from being used much for slipcovers. As thin fabrics woven from smooth-surfaced yarn, 100 percent synthetics tend to be so slippery you'd have difficulty keeping them in place. As thicker fabrics woven from nappy-surfaced yarn, 100 percent synthetics are usually too bulky for a home sewing machine.

The slipcover fabrics from which you are most likely to make your selection are these:

Bedsheets. Available in four sizes: twin (5 square yards), full (6 square yards), queen (7 square yards), king (8½ square yards). Smooth-surfaced percale sheets have more threads per square inch and therefore more strength than coarser-surfaced muslin. For slipcovers, buy flat (unfitted) bedsheets.

More threads per square inch give percale sheets more strength than muslin ones.

PERCALE SHEET
50% POLYESTER
50% COMBED COTTON

PERMANENT PRESSED MUSLIN SHEET

FULL SIZE FLAT SHEET

Calico. See Percale.

Chambray. Colored warp, white filling yarn. Polished surface, often printed in stripes or checks. Plain weave.

Chintz. Lightweight cotton glazed on one side. Tightly woven. Buy the best grade you can afford; inexpensive chintz tends to tear.

Corduroy. Ribs or "wales" created by shearing loops of pile-type weave. Also available without wales. Pile runs in one direction. Buy only lightweight for sewing on home machine.

Cotton damask. Woven, raised designs of figures or flowers. Often reversible. Somewhat slippery. Ravels easily—plan ¾-inch rather than ½-inch seam allowances.

Cotton/polyester. The polyester fiber adds soil and wrinkle resistance. Sometimes the weave is twill (adds strength), sometimes plain (as with bedsheets).

Cotton taffeta. Fine cotton; holds shape well. Slight sheen on both sides.

Cretonne. Cotton or linen—or blends. Often floral prints.

Denim. High durability, low cost. Available mostly in solid colors; some prints and two-tones. Often looks as good with reverse (lighter) side out.

Duck. Same characteristics as denim, but slightly less durability because of plain weave instead of twill. One weight lighter than sailcloth.

Linen. Woven of flax, wrinkles badly unless very tightly fitted. Soils easily and cleans easily. Bulkier than cotton. Aristocratic look reflected in high price.

Linen/cotton. Cotton reduces wrinkles and price; linen contributes texture and crispness.

Muslin. Cotton or cotton/polyester with nappy, dull effect. Available as bedsheets and as bolt fabric. Sometimes used underneath slipcovers as upholstery fabric and to line skirts. Many weights.

Percale. Often called calico (known for its figured patterns in bright colors). Smooth, tightly woven. Sold as bedsheets or on bolts.

Polished cotton. Heavier than chintz, less sheen.

Poplin. Medium-weight fabric, often cotton, with slight ribbed effect.

Sailcloth. Casual look, one weight lighter than canvas, one heavier than duck. Excellent for outdoor slipcovers, but test to make sure your home machine can sew through multiple layers.

Sateen. Cotton, shiny but not slippery, often printed in stripes and bright colors. Sometimes used to line slipcover skirts.

Ticking. Cotton or linen or blend, often used to cover mattresses and pillows. Usually striped.

Velvet, velveteen. Pile fabric with cut loops; level or sculptured. Soft feel. Plain and patterned. Pile usually runs in one direction.

How to Calculate Yardage

We offer you two choices in calculating yardage. On pages 42–43 is the yardage estimate chart—use it for looking up approximate yardage for standard furniture types. On pages 48–51 are the measurement lists—use them if you prefer to determine exact yardage or if your furniture is unusual.

Terms used on chart & lists

Following is a discussion of terms used on the yardage chart and measurement lists.

Bolt fabric, running yards. Bolt fabric—sometimes folded in half lengthwise, sometimes not—comes wrapped around a rectangle or tube of cardboard. Most bolt fabrics suitable for slipcovers are 45 to 54 inches wide; 48 and 54-inch widths are the most common. A few fabrics less than 45 inches wide are suitable for slipcovers, but because so many of the measurements and techniques in this book would have to be changed to accommodate narrow fabrics, we don't recommend using them.

Slipcover fabrics are usually 45, 48, or 54 inches wide.

Bedsheets offer variety and economy for slipcovers.

You buy all bolt fabrics by the length measured in yards (called "yardage" or "running yards"). Eight running yards of bolt fabric, for instance, is 8 yards long whether the width is 48 inches or 54 inches.

Bedsheets, square yards. Bedsheets may not last as long as heavier fabrics, nor stay as crisp looking, but they are inexpensive, easy to sew, and easily laundered. Like bolt fabrics, they can be railroaded or vertically run (see below). Yardage for bedsheets is figured in square yards, rather than running yards.

Square-yard requirements presume that you will buy flat finished sheets. If you find you need a few extra inches on a flat finished sheet, you can always rip out the hem; or you can buy matching pillowcases for small slipcover pieces such as front arm sections.

To slipcover most furniture pieces requires two different sheet sizes. For a fully upholstered armchair, for example, you'll probably need a full sheet (6 square yards) and a twin sheet (5 square yards).

When using the measurement lists, after you convert measurements in inches to running yards, you multiply running yards by the key number—1½ —to get square yards.

Railroading. With this technique you align fabric along the width of your furniture, usually resulting in two principal advantages—you need fewer seams and you use less fabric.

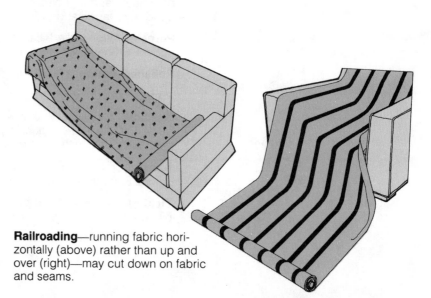

Railroading—running fabric horizontally (above) rather than up and over (right)—may cut down on fabric and seams.

If your piece of furniture is wider than the fabric is (often the case with love seats, sofabeds, and sofas), railroading lets you eliminate seams on the outside and inside back, the deck, and the furniture's front (for illustration of terms, see page 48). Railroading's saving of fabric can be substantial— approximately 10 percent for a skirtless, fully upholstered armchair and 15 percent for a skirted sofa 84 inches wide, compared with the method of draping fabric vertically.

You can railroad a majority of the fabrics on the market. Why can't you railroad the rest? Because prints showing people, animals, buildings, trees, and flowers with stems look strange turned sideways. And because velvets and corduroys have pile—tiny, stand-up threads that tend to lean in one direction. Railroading directs the pile toward the left or right arm of a chair or sofa, rather than up and down, and this changes the color effect. Nor will you want to railroad plaids or stripes when their visual thrust side to side would make your piece of furniture look lower and wider than you wish.

Skirt. The fabric panel that surrounds the base of a piece of furniture and drapes to the floor is called a skirt, and it greatly improves the appearance of many pieces of furniture. Not only does it give a finished look, but a skirt

Some designs require that fabric be run over furniture vertically.

also helps keep the slipcover snug and eliminates the need to secure the slipcover to the frame. Skirts require additional yardage, though.

There are four basic skirt designs: straight or tailored, gathered, box pleated, and knife pleated (from simplest to most complicated to construct). The yardage estimate chart and measurement lists assume that all skirts are self-lined; you'll find sewing instructions on pages 88–93.

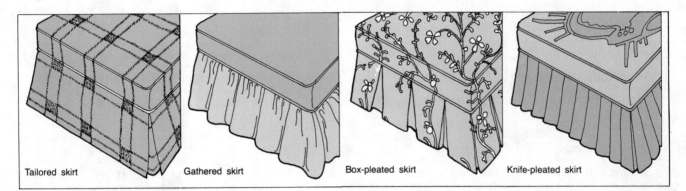

| Tailored skirt | Gathered skirt | Box-pleated skirt | Knife-pleated skirt |

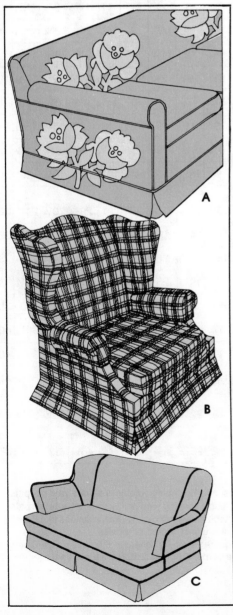

Motif repeat. Some fabrics repeat prominent designs—a building, a flower, a group of people—which you must center on various parts of your furniture in order to achieve a sense of balance. Other repeats—stripes, checks, plaids, rows of motifs—need to be matched up as you pin the fabric pieces together before sewing. If the motifs of your fabric repeat with greater frequency than every 3 inches, you needn't buy extra fabric for centering or matching. At the bottom of the chart and lists you'll find information on how much extra fabric you'll need for larger repeats.

Welt. Also at the bottom of the chart and lists is guidance in determining the extra amount of fabric needed to make welt, the fabric-wrapped cord that defines a slipcover's seams. Though you can create a no-welt slipcover (see page 88), traditional slipcovers, like traditional upholstery, gain a finished look from welt. You can make matching welt from the slipcover fabric or use a contrasting fabric to highlight the seams. Directions for making welt are on pages 83–85.

Using the Yardage Estimate Chart

You'll find that the yardage estimate chart on pages 42–43 shows at a glance, for both bolt fabrics and bedsheets, how much yardage to buy for 23 types of furniture, whether or not you want to add a skirt.

The chart's figures, of course, can only be approximate; there are almost as many variations in furniture and fabric as in the human form. To be safe, buy an extra ½ yard for a chair, a full yard for a larger piece of furniture. Keep in mind, too, that 54-inch-wide fabric yields more usable scrap than 45-inch-wide fabric. You'll use this scrap for testing and for making front arm sections, shoulders, arm protectors, cushion boxing, and throw pillows. You'll also want to store some fabric in case you have to replace a section damaged later on.

A Large florals need centering.
B Plaids must be matched.
C Contrasting welt highlights seams.

YARDAGE ESTIMATE CHART

This chart is an approximate guide for estimating yards needed. For more precise calculations, see the Measurement Lists, pages 48-51.

		45" to 54" Bolt Fabrics (Running Yards)						Bedsheets—Flat (Square Yards)					
		Railroaded			Vertically Run			Railroaded			Vertically Run		
		No Skirt	Tailored Skirt	Other Skirts	No Skirt	Tailored Skirt	Other Skirts	No Skirt	Tailored Skirt	Other Skirts	No Skirt	Tailored Skirt	Other Skirts
A	Standard Ottoman (up to 22 by 22 inches)	1½	2½	4½	1½	2½	4½	2¼	3¾	6¾	2¼	3¾	6¾
B	Oversized Ottoman (23 by 23 inches to 27 by 27 inches)	2	3½	5½	2	3½	5½	3	5¼	8¼	3	5¼	8¼
C	Dining Room Chair	2	—	—	2	—	—	3	—	—	3	—	—
D	Armless Boudoir Chair (10-inch skirt)	2	4	8	2	4	8	3	6	12	3	6	12
E	Boudoir Armchair (10-inch skirt)	5	7¼	11¾	6½	8	11	7½	11	17¾	9¾	12	16½
F	Barrelback Chair	5	7¼	11¾	6½	8	11	7½	11	17¾	9¾	12	16½
G	Platform Rocker	5¼	7½	12	5¾	7½	11¼	8	11¼	18	8¾	11¼	17
H	Fully Upholstered Armchair	5¼	7½	12	5¾	7½	11¼	8	11¼	18	8¾	11¼	17
I	Chair with Removable Back Cushion	6¾	9	13½	8¼	9¾	12¾	10¼	13½	20¼	12½	14¾	19¼
J	Low-back Wing Chair	5¼	7½	12	5¾	7½	11¼	8	11¼	18	8¾	11¼	17
K	High-back Wing Chair (10-inch skirt)	7	10	16	9	11	15	10½	15	24	13½	16½	22½
L	Chaise Longue with No Cushions	5¼	8¾	15¾	6¾	9½	13	8	11¼	18	8¾	11¼	17
M	Chaise Longue with Removable Deck Cushion	9½	12¼	17¾	11	13¼	17¾	14¼	18½	26¾	16½	20	26¾
N	Chaise Longue with Removable Deck and Back Cushions	11¼	14	19½	13½	16¼	21¾	17	21	29¼	20¼	24½	32¾
O	2-Cushion Love Seat (to 60 inches wide)	9¾	12½	18¼	12	14¼	19	14¾	18¾	27½	18	21½	28½
P	2-Cushion Sofa (to 84 inches wide)	12¾	16¾	24¾	16¼	19½	26	19¼	25¼	37¼	24½	29¼	39
Q	2-Cushion Sofabed (to 84 inches wide)	12¾	16¾	24¾	16¼	19½	26	19¼	25¼	37¼	24½	29¼	39
R	2-Cushion Wing Sofa (to 84 inches wide)	13½	17½	25½	16¾	20	26½	20¼	26¼	38¼	25¼	30	39¾
S	3-Cushion Sofa (to 84 inches wide)	14¼	18¼	26¼	17	20¼	26¾	21½	27½	39½	25½	30½	40¼
T	3-Cushion Sofabed (to 84 inches wide)	14¼	18¼	26¼	17	20¼	26¾	21½	27½	39½	25½	30½	40¼
U	3-Cushion Wing Sofa (to 84 inches wide)	15	19	27	17¾	21	27½	22½	28½	40½	26¾	31½	41¼
V	2-Cushion Sofa (to 84 inches wide) with 2 Removable Back Cushions	15¾	19¾	27¾	19	22¼	28¾	23¾	29¾	41¾	28½	33½	43¼
W	3-Cushion Sofa (to 84 inches wide) with 3 Removable Back Cushions	18¾	22¾	30¾	22	25¼	31¾	28¼	34¼	46¼	33	38	47¾

EXTRA FABRIC NEEDED

- If motif repeats every 3 to 12 inches, add ¾ running yard or 1¼ square yards for chairs, 1 running yard or 1½ square yards for love seats and chaise longues, 1½ running yards or 2¼ square yards for sofas and sofabeds. Double these amounts for repeats over 12 inches.
- For welt, add ¾ running yard or 1¼ square yards for chairs, 1¼ running yards or 2 square yards for love seats and chaise longues, 1¾ running yards or 2¾ square yards for sofas and sofabeds up to 84 inches (7 feet) wide.
- For arm protectors, add ½ running yard or ¾ square yard per pair.
- For throw pillows, add 1 running yard or 1½ square yards per pair.
- All arm furniture pieces have removable deck cushions and 6-inch-high, self-lined skirts unless stated otherwise.
- Twin sheet = 5 square yards. Full sheet = 6 square yards. Queen sheet = 7 square yards. King sheet = 8½ square yards.

The following basic furniture styles are illustrated to help you estimate the amount of fabric you'll need. Your furniture may vary slightly; choose the illustration that most closely resembles the piece of furniture you plan to slipcover.

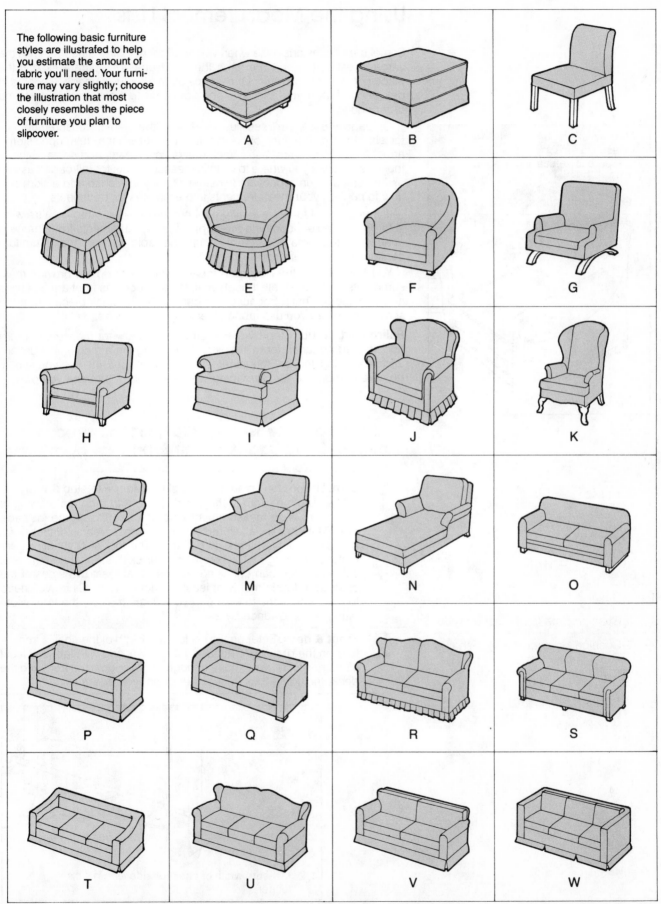

A

B

C

D

E

F

G

H

I

J

K

L

M

N

O

P

Q

R

S

T

U

V

W

Using the Measurement Lists

Sometimes occasions arise when you need to measure rather than use the yardage estimate chart. Perhaps the chart doesn't illustrate exactly the piece of furniture you have. Or perhaps a manufacturer needs 3 months to deliver the fabric you choose—and you want to make doubly sure you order enough.

On pages 48–51 you'll see illustrated, fill-in-the-blanks measurement lists for six types of furniture often slipcovered—ottomans, fully upholstered armchairs, wing chairs, barrelback chairs, love seats, and sofas. Each of these lists shows you where to write in measurements for railroaded as well as for vertically run slipcovers (whether or not you wish to add a skirt) and how to convert your measurements into estimates for bedsheets.

If your piece of furniture is different from the one illustrated—if it's a wing sofa, for example—combine the applicable measurements from the wing chair and the sofa lists. You should be able to find most furniture configurations by referring to the lists.

You'll notice that the illustrated measurement lists do not provide measurements for such small, though vital, fabric pieces as front arm sections and shoulders. That's because you can cut these small pieces from the scraps, provided you use fabric at least 45 inches wide.

Railroaded fabric. Step-by-step instructions follow for measuring a fully upholstered armchair for railroading. By reading the armchair instructions and examining the six measurement lists on pages 48–51, you should be able to measure for railroading whatever kind of furniture you own.

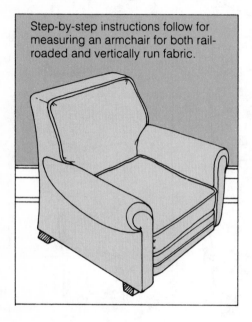

Step-by-step instructions follow for measuring an armchair for both rail-roaded and vertically run fabric.

Step-by-step: Measuring a fully upholstered armchair for railroading bolt fabrics or bedsheets

1 **Skirt.** (If you don't plan to add a skirt, begin with step 2.)

Measure the width of the chair's front, A to B on the drawing (if the chair's side measurement is larger, use that figure instead). Add 24 inches for a tailored skirt with corner pleats, 72 inches for box pleats, knife pleats, or gathers. (The four skirt variations are pictured on page 41.) Assuming your skirt is 6 inches high and self-lined, you can cut skirt sections for at least two sides of the chair from fabric that is at least 45 inches wide. Since you need four skirt sections to surround your chair, multiply the front width plus pleat allowance by 2.

2 **Front & deck.** Enter on the list just the width of the chair's front, A to B on the drawing. Because you are working with fabric at least 45 inches wide, you'll have enough to cover both the front and the deck, including tuck-in, whether or not you add a skirt.

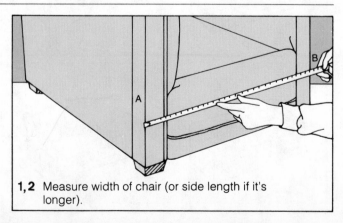

1,2 Measure width of chair (or side length if it's longer).

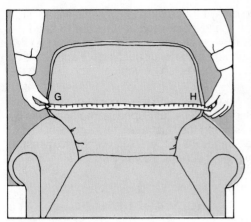

3 Inside back's greatest width.

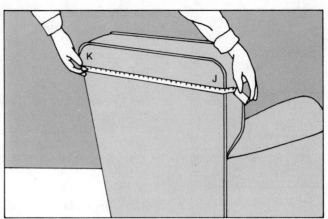

4 Outside back's greatest width.

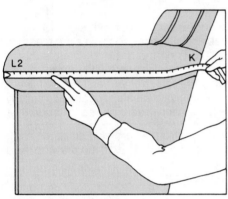

5 Outside arm's length.

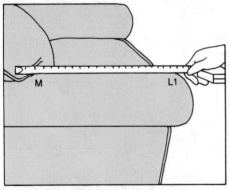

6 Inside arm's length (no skirt).

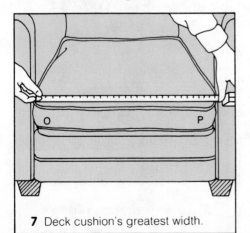

7 Deck cushion's greatest width.

3 **Inside back.** Measure widest part of chair's inside back, G to H. Add 4 inches of fabric to work with.

4 **Outside back.** Measure greatest width of chair's outside back, J to K. Add 4 inches of fabric to work with.

5 **Outside arms.** Measure length of chair's outside arm, L2 to K. If you plan a skirt, this measurement gives you enough fabric to cover both outside and inside arm (if no skirt, outside arm only). Add 4 inches of fabric to work with. Double the total because chair has two arms.

6 **Inside arms—*No skirt.*** If you *don't* plan to add a skirt, measure length of inside arm, L1 to M. Add 4 inches of fabric to work with. Double the total because chair has two arms.

7 **Deck cushion.** Measure widest part of deck cushion along cushion edge, O to P. This gives you enough fabric to cover cushion's top side and its bottom side. Add 4 inches of fabric to work with.

8 **Back cushion.** If your chair has a removable back cushion, repeat step 7 and double the measurement. This gives you enough fabric for removable back cushion's front and reverse, and for both its and the deck cushion's boxing. (If you have only a deck cushion, you can piece together its boxing out of scrap.)

9 **Extras.** Add to your list any fabric needed for extras such as motif repeats, welts, and throw pillows.

Total. Add your totals in inches from steps 1 through 9. Divide by 36. The result is the number of running yards of bolt fabric to buy for railroading a fully upholstered armchair.

If you prefer to use bedsheets, multiply the running yards you calculated for bolt fabrics by the key number—1½. The result is the approximate number of square yards of bedsheets you need. (For a discussion of using bedsheets, see page 40.)

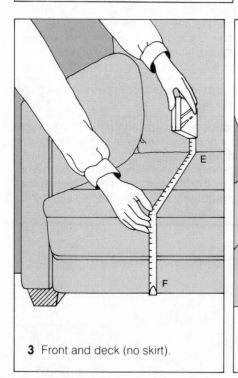

1 Skirt height from floor.

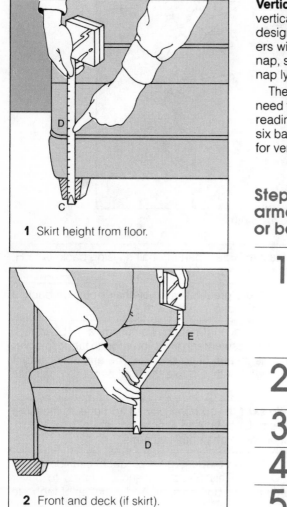

2 Front and deck (if skirt).

Vertically run fabric. You'll find many fabrics with designs that are best run vertically—up and over the arms and back of your furniture to keep the designs upright. These designs may be stripes or plaids, they may be flowers with stems, they may be people, animals, or buildings. Fabrics with a nap, such as velvet and corduroy, should also be vertically run to keep the nap lying in one direction.

The following method shows how to estimate the amount of fabric you'll need to make a vertically run slipcover for a fully upholstered armchair. By reading the instructions and examining the illustrated measurement lists of six basic furniture categories on pages 48–51, you'll know how to measure for vertically run fabric, whatever kind of furniture you own.

Step-by-step: Measuring a fully upholstered armchair for vertically run bolt fabrics or bedsheets.

1 Skirt. (If you don't plan to add a skirt, begin with step 3.)

To estimate how much fabric you'll need to cut a skirt, measure skirt height from the floor, C to D on the drawing. Double this to make the skirt self-lined. Add 1 inch for seam allowance.

For a tailored skirt, multiply the total (13 inches for a self-lined, 6-inch skirt) by 4. For box pleats, knife pleats, or gathers, multiply the total by 8. (The four skirt variations are pictured on page 41.)

2 Front & deck—*If skirt.* Measure from where skirt starts on chair front to where deck meets inside back, D to E on the drawing. Add 5 inches for seams and tuck-in.

3 Front & deck—*No skirt.* Measure from bottom of chair up front to rear of deck, F to E. Add 5 inches for seams and tuck-in.

4 Inside back. Measure height of chair's inside back to rear of top, E to I. Add 7 inches for seams and tuck-in.

5 Outside back—*If skirt.* Measure partial height of chair's outside back, D to I. Add 4 inches of fabric to work with.

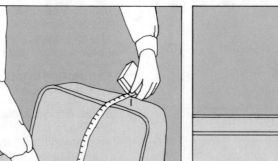

3 Front and deck (no skirt).   **4** Inside back to rear of top.   **5** Outside back height (if skirt).

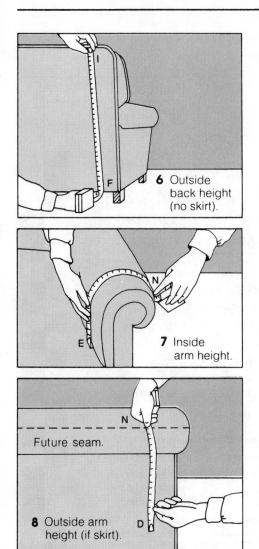

6 Outside back height (no skirt).

7 Inside arm height.

Future seam.

8 Outside arm height (if skirt).

6 **Outside back—*No skirt.*** Measure height of chair's outside back, I to F. Add 4 inches of fabric to work with.

7 **Inside arms.** Measure height of chair's inside arm from deck to imaginary line (future seam) halfway around arm's curve, E to N. Add 5 inches for seams and tuck-in. Double the total because chair has two arms.

8 **Outside arms—*If skirt.*** Measure partial height of chair's outside arm, from skirtline of chair to imaginary line (future seam) halfway around arm's curve, D to N. Add 4 inches of material to work with. Double the total because chair has two arms.

9 **Outside arms—*No skirt.*** Measure height of chair's outside arm from bottom of chair to imaginary line (future seam), halfway around arm's curve, F to N. Add 4 inches of fabric to work with. Double the total because chair has two arms.

10 **Deck cushion.** Measure deck cushion length along cushion edge, Q to R. This gives you enough fabric to cover cushion's top side and its bottom side if cushion's *width* is 23 inches or less (double length if width is more than 23 inches). Add 4 inches of fabric to work with.

11 **Deck cushion boxing.** Measure cushion boxing height, S to T. Add 2 inches for seam allowance. Triple the total. This gives you enough fabric to add a zipper in back of cushion.

12 **Back cushion.** If your chair has a removable back cushion, repeat steps 10 and 11.

13 **Extras.** Add to your list fabric needed for extras such as motif repeats, welt, and throw pillows.

Total. Add your total in inches from steps 1 through 13. Divide by 36. The result is the number of running yards of bolt fabric to buy for vertically run slipcovering of a fully upholstered armchair.

If you prefer to use bedsheets, multiply the running yards you calculated for bolt fabrics by the key number—1½. The result is the approximate number of square yards of bedsheets you need. (For a discussion of using bedsheets, see page 40.)

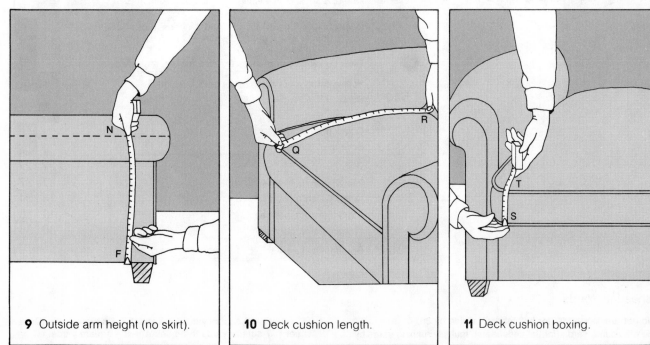

9 Outside arm height (no skirt).   **10** Deck cushion length.   **11** Deck cushion boxing.

MEASUREMENT LISTS

To use these measurement lists for precise calculations—in inches—of fabric needed, fill in the blocks that apply to railroaded or vertically run fabric. Then convert inches to running yards (see below).

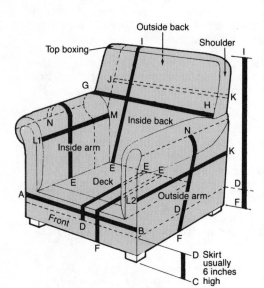

Top boxing
Outside back
Shoulder
Inside back
Inside arm
Deck
Front
Outside arm

D Skirt usually 6 inches high
C

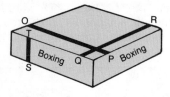

O R
T
Boxing Q P Boxing
S

FULLY UPHOLSTERED ARMCHAIR

		Railroaded	Vertically Run
Skirt	Railroaded 6 to 8-inch self-lined skirt (tailored)—A to B. Add 40 inches. Multiply by 2.		
	Railroaded 6 to 8-inch self-lined skirt (box or knife pleated, or gathered)—A to B. Add 98 inches. Multiply by 2.		
	Vertically run skirt (tailored)—C to D. Double, then add 1 inch. Multiply by 5.		
	Vertically run skirt (box or knife pleated, or gathered)—C to D. Double, then add 1 inch. Multiply by 9.		
Front & Deck	Front width—A to B.		
	Partial front to rear of deck (if skirt)—D to E. Add 5 inches.		
	Front to rear of deck (if no skirt)—F to E. Add 5 inches.		
Inside Back	Widest inside back width—G to H. Add 4 inches.		
	Inside back height to rear of top—E to I. Add 7 inches.		
Outside Back	Widest outside back width—J to K. Add 4 inches.		
	Partial outside back height (if skirt)—D to I. Add 4 inches.		
	Outside back height (if no skirt)—F to I. Add 7 inches.		
Inside Arms	Inside arm length (if no skirt)—L1 to M. Add 4 inches. Multiply by 2.		
	Inside arm height—E to N. Add 5 inches. Multiply by 2.		
Outside Arms	Outside arm length—L2 to K. Add 4 inches. Multiply by 2.		
	Partial outside arm height (if skirt)—D to N. Add 4 inches. Multiply by 2.		
	Outside arm height (if no skirt)—F to N. Add 4 inches. Multiply by 2.		
Deck Cushion	Greatest deck cushion width—O to P. Add 4 inches. (For 45-inch fabric, double total if greatest *length*—Q to R—is more than 21 inches.)		
	Deck cushion boxing—cushion width, O to P, plus cushion length, Q to R, plus 4 inches (or plus 10 inches for L or T-shaped cushion).		
	Deck cushion length—Q to R. Add 4 inches. (For 45-inch fabric, double total if greatest *width*—O to P—is more than 21 inches.)		
	Deck cushion boxing—S to T. Add 2 inches. Multiply by 3.		
Back Cushion (if removable)	Follow same procedures as for deck cushion.		
	Cushion		
	Boxing		
	Cushion		
	Boxing		
Extras	Welt.	27	27
	3 to 12-inch motif repeat.	27	27
	13 to 24-inch motif repeat.	54	54
	Arm protectors, per pair.	18	18
	Throw pillows, per pair.	36	36
Total	Grand total in inches.		

Inches Into Yards

- To get running yards (for bolt fabrics), divide by 36.
- To get square yards (for flat bedsheets), multiply running yards by 1½.
- Twin sheet = 5 square yards. Full sheet = 6 square yards. Queen sheet = 7 square yards. King sheet = 8½ square yards.

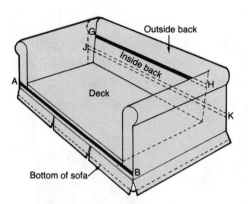

Outside back

Inside back

Deck

A

G

J

F

H

K

B

Bottom of sofa

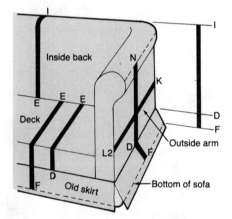

Inside back

Deck

N

K

E E E

L2

D

F

F

D

I

I

D

F

Outside arm

Bottom of sofa

Old skirt

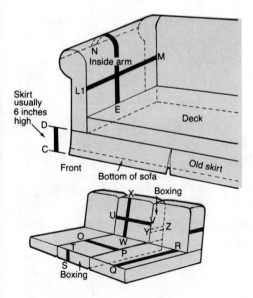

N

Inside arm

M

L1

E

Deck

Skirt usually 6 inches high

D

C

Front

Bottom of sofa

Old skirt

X

Boxing

U

N

V

Z

O

Y

W

P

R

S

T

Boxing

Q

THREE-CUSHION SOFA
(With 3 Removable Back Cushions)

		Railroaded	Vertically Run
Skirt	Railroaded 6 to 8-inch self-lined skirt (tailored)—A to B. Add 48 inches.		
	Railroaded 6 to 8-inch self-lined skirt (box or knife pleated, or gathered)—A to B. Add 144 inches.		
	Vertically run skirt (tailored)—C to D. Double, then add 1 inch. Multiply by 8.		
	Vertically run skirt (box or knife pleated, or gathered)—C to D. Double, then add 1 inch. Multiply by 16.		
Front & Deck	Front width—A to B.		
	Partial front to rear of deck (if skirt)—D to E. Add 5 inches. Multiply by 2.		
	Front to rear of deck (if no skirt)—F to E. Add 5 inches. Multiply by 2.		
Inside Back	Inside back width—G to H. Add 4 inches.		
	Inside back height to rear of top—E to I. Add 7 inches. Multiply by 2.		
Outside Back	Outside back width—J to K. Add 4 inches.		
	Partial outside back height (if skirt)—D to I. Add 4 inches. Multiply by 2.		
	Outside back height (if no skirt)—F to I. Add 4 inches. Multiply by 2.		
Inside Arms	Inside arm length (if no skirt)—L1 to M. Add 4 inches. Multiply by 2.		
	Inside arm height—E to N. Add 5 inches. Multiply by 2.		
Outside Arms	Outside arm length—L2 to K. Add 4 inches. Multiply by 2.		
	Partial outside arm height (if skirt)—D to N. Add 4 inches. Multiply by 2.		
	Outside arm height (if no skirt)—F to N. Add 4 inches. Multiply by 2.		
Deck Cushions	Greatest deck cushion width—O to P. Add 4 inches (for 45-inch fabric, double total if greatest *length*—Q to R—is more than 21 inches).		
	Deck cushion boxing—cushion width, O to P, plus cushion length—Q to R, plus 4 inches (or, plus 10 inches for L or T-shaped cushions).		
	Deck cushion length—Q to R. Add 4 inches (for 45-inch fabric, double total if greatest width—O to P—is more than 21 inches). Multiply by 2.		
	Deck cushion boxing—S to T. Add 2 inches. Multiply by 6.		
Back Cushions (if removable)	Follow same procedures as for deck cushions. Cushion.		
	Boxing.		
	Cushion.		
	Boxing.		
Extras	Welt.	99	99
	3 to 12-inch motif repeat.	54	54
	13 to 24-inch motif repeat.	108	108
	Arm protectors, per pair.	18	18
	Throw pillows, per pair.	36	36
Total	Grand total in inches.		

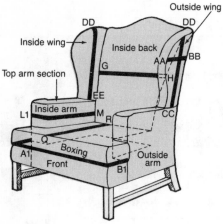

	Railroaded	Vertically Run

T-DECK WING CHAIR

Same as Fully Upholstered Armchair, with these exceptions:

		Railroaded	Vertically Run
Add Wings	Outside wing length—AA to BB. Add 5 inches. Multiply by 2.		
	Outside wing height—CC to DD. Add 4 inches.		
	Inside wing height to rear of top—EE to DD. Add 4 inches.		
Inside Back	Add 6 inches (instead of 4 inches) to greatest width of inside back—G to H.		
Deck Cushion	Deck T-cushion length—Q to R. Add 4 inches. Multiply by 2.		
Front & T-Deck	Front width—A1 to B1 (instead of A to B). Add 4 inches.		
Inside Arm	Inside arm length (if no skirt)—L1 to M. Add 4 inches. Multiply by 2.		

BARRELBACK CHAIR

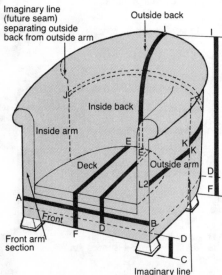

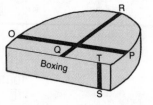

		Railroaded	Vertically Run
Skirt	Railroaded 6 to 8-inch self-lined skirt (tailored)—A to B. Add 24 inches. Multiply by 2.		
	Railroaded 6 to 8-inch self-lined skirt (box or knife pleated, or gathered)—A to B. Add 72 inches. Multiply by 2.		
	Vertically run skirt (tailored)—C to D. Double, then add 1 inch. Multiply by 4.		
	Vertically run skirt (box or knife pleated, or gathered)—C to D. Double, then add 1 inch. Multiply by 8.		
Front & Deck	Front width—A to B.		
	Partial front to rear of deck (if skirt)—D to E. Add 5 inches.		
	Front to rear of deck (if no skirt)—F to E. Add 6 inches.		
Inside Back	Inside back height to rear of top—E to I. Add 7 inches. Multiply by 2.		
Outside Back	Greatest outside back width (if skirt)—J to K. Add 4 inches.		
	Greatest outside back width (if no skirt)—J to K. Add 4 inches. Multiply by 2.		
	Outside back height (if skirt)—D to I. Add 4 inches. Multiply by 2.		
	Outside back height (if no skirt)—F to I. Add 4 inches. Multiply by 2.		
Outside Arms	Outside arm length (if skirt)—K to L2. Add 4 inches. Multiply by 2.		
	Outside arm length (if no skirt)—K to L2. Add 4 inches. Multiply by 4.		
Deck Cushion	Greatest deck cushion width—O to P. Add 4 inches.		
	Deck cushion length—Q to R. Add 4 inches.		
	Deck cushion boxing—S to T. Add 2 inches.		
Extras	Welt.	27	27
	3 to 12-inch motif repeat.	18	18
	13 to 24-inch motif repeat.	36	36
	Arm protectors, per pair.	18	18
	Throw pillows, per pair.	36	36
Total	Grand total in inches.		

Inches into Yards

- To get running yards (for bolt fabrics), divide by 36. To get square yards (for flat bedsheets), multiply running yards by 1½.

- Twin sheet = 5 square yards. Full sheet = 6 square yards. Queen sheet = 7 square yards. King sheet = 8½ square yards.

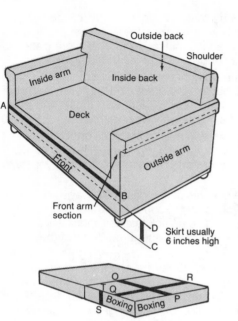

Outside back

Shoulder

Inside arm

Inside back

Deck

A

Front

Outside arm

B

Front arm section

D

C

Skirt usually 6 inches high

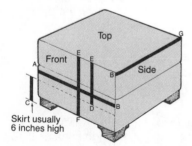

O   R
T Q
Boxing   Boxing
S   P

TWO-CUSHION LOVE SEAT
Same as Three-Cushion Sofa, with these exceptions:

		Railroaded	Vertically Run
Skirt	Railroaded 6 to 8-inch self-lined skirt (tailored)—A to B. Add 36 inches.		
	Railroaded 6 to 8-inch self-lined skirt (box or knife pleated, or gathered)—A to B. Add 108 inches.		
	Vertically run skirt (tailored)—C to D. Double, then add 1 inch. Multiply by 6.		
	Vertically run skirt (box or knife-pleated, or gathered)— C to D. Double, then add 1 inch. Multiply by 12.		
Deck Cushions	Greatest deck cushion width—O to P. Add 4 inches (for 45-inch fabric, double total if greatest *length*—Q to R—is more than 21 inches). Multiply by 2.		
	Deck cushion boxing—cushion width, O to P plus cushion length, Q to R, plus 4 inches (or, plus 10 inches for L or T-shaped cushions).		
	Deck cushion length—Q to R. Add 4 inches (for 45-inch fabric, double total if greatest *width*—O to P—is more than 21 inches). Multiply by 2.		
	Deck cushion boxing—S to T. Add 2 inches. Multiply by 6.		
Back Cushions (if removable)	Follow same procedures as for deck cushions.		
	Cushion.		
	Boxing.		
	Cushion.		
	Boxing.		
Extras	Welt.	63	63
	3 to 12-inch motif repeat.	36	36
	13 to 24-inch motif repeat.	72	72
	Arm protectors, per pair.	18	18
	Throw pillows, per pair.	36	36

OTTOMAN

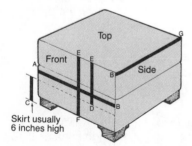

Top
G
Front
E   E
A
B   Side
C
B
D
F

Skirt usually 6 inches high

		Railroaded	Vertically Run
Skirt	Railroaded 6-inch skirt (tailored)—A to B. Add 24 inches. Multiply by 2.		
	Railroaded 6-inch self-lined skirt (box or knife pleated, gathered)—A to B. Add 72 inches. Multiply by 2.		
	Vertically run skirt (tailored)—C to D. Double, then add 1 inch. Multiply by 4.		
	Vertically run skirt (box or knife pleated, or gathered)— C to D. Double, then add 1 inch. Multiply by 8.		
Front & Top	Front width—A to B. Add 4 inches. Multiply by 2.		
	Top or side length—E to G. Add 4 inches.		
	Partial front height (if skirt)—D to E. Add 4 inches. Multiply by 2.		
	Front height (if no skirt)—F to E. Add 4 inches. Multiply by 2.		
Extras	Welt.	18	18
	3 to 12-inch motif repeat.	18	18
	13 to 24-inch motif repeat.	36	36
Total	Grand total in inches.		

MAKING THE SLIPCOVER

This book is intended to help you create, on your first try, slipcovers you can be proud of. That's why it emphasizes the simplest techniques possible. Certain alternate approaches that may demand more patience or sewing skill but will result in a snugger fit are described also.

Furniture has its mavericks: the "attached pillowback" sofa whose back cushions are not quite detachable; the chair whose arms are but extensions of its back. You will read how to deal with these and other nonconformists as well as with their more orthodox brethren.

A Lawson-style, fully upholstered armchair is about as orthodox as you can get. It was picked as this book's star to show in detail how to create a standard slipcover, from the time you start to measure to the time you gaze at your chair in pride.

Take time now to examine the features of this chair (see page 48). It has a square deck cushion (not T-shaped or round in the front), arms that come all the way to the front of the chair, a back that has shoulders and top boxing, and a spring-edge deck with a crevice at the front of the inside arm.

Now look at your piece of furniture. It may be an attached pillowback sofa whose back cushions are not quite detachable; a chair with "wings" that are extensions of its back; a chair or sofa with a T-shaped deck. Such variations in construction features will require changes in the slipcover instructions we give for our fully upholstered armchair. By following the instructions for the armchair, and using the variations where they apply to your furniture, you'll find the task goes faster than you thought it would.

The process of making a slipcover, no matter how detailed it seems, reduces to four main steps: cutting individual fabric sections roughly to size (called "blocking out"), pinning these sections together on the sofa or chair (called "pin-fitting"), trimming the sections to within a half-inch of their intended seams, and stitching those seams on your sewing machine. This book follows those steps in sequence, then gives directions for welt, skirts, and cushions.

Patching upholstery. If your old upholstery is ripped, you should patch it so it won't tear further once it's hidden from view. Sheeting or a clean rag affixed by fabric glue (available at most fabric shops) works fine. If the tear is large, you may need to restuff with cotton or polyester batting and whipstitch the frayed edges together before patching.

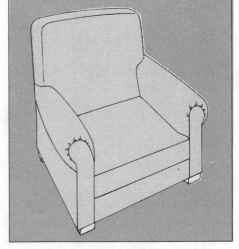

Blocking out instructions are based on this fully upholstered armchair.

Blocking Out

"Blocking out" describes the technique for cutting bolt fabrics or bedsheets down to manageable size, giving you enough extra cloth to pin seams together and, where needed, tuck fabric edges into crevices. A fully upholstered armchair takes 11 blocked-out fabric sections; a two-cushion, 60-inch-wide love seat takes the same number of sections if railroaded, four more if the fabric is vertically run—draped up and over the love seat's arms and back.

Not all fabric sections are blocked out. For cushion boxing (the strip that connects the cushion's bottom and top), welt, and the furniture's skirt, you must measure precisely, draw chalk lines on the cloth, and cut the sections out on the floor or on a large table.

For most fabric sections, however, blocking out saves a great deal of time; it also eliminates the confusion that plagues attempts to chalk all sections onto the fabric before cutting them out. Chalking attempts approach the herculean when it comes to working with motifs that must be centered, or stripes or plaids needing to be matched.

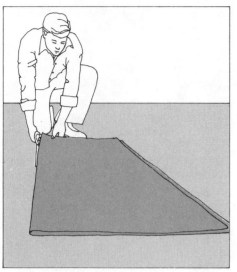

One way to cut fabric is to cut stroke-by-stroke on a flat surface.

Cutting fabric

Good shears can eliminate shredded cloth and shredded nerves. Before you start, make sure the blades are sharp (try them on a fabric swatch). The cutting edges should touch—listen for a slight whistling sound as they come together.

One critical step in blocking out a slipcover is forming a straight, even fold at the point where you want to cut the fabric. Once the fold is made, you can move the fabric to a large table or the floor, check for straightness, and cut along the fold in the usual manner. Or you can borrow the professional's technique of cutting down through the vertically held fold in a single, gliding stroke.

If you're cutting fabric with a ribbed or nubby texture, cut on a flat surface. Particularly on long cuts, it's easier to lay the fabric out, align lengthwise edges, and cut a blade length at a time. If you're using a light to medium-weight fabric and your shears are very sharp, the single-stroke method will give a clean, straight cut. Try both methods on similar fabric to decide which will work best. If you're left-handed, use the hand opposite that named.

How to form a cutting fold. Whichever way you're cutting—one stroke at a time on a flat surface, or with a single vertical stroke—here's how to fold your fabric for cutting. (For most sections, blocking out begins with the fabric folded lengthwise, in which case the "top edge" of the fabric refers to the lengthwise fold.)

With your left hand, grasp the top edge of the fabric at its end; with your right hand, grasp the top edge of the fabric at the point where you wish to cut. Use your left hand to bring the top edges of the fabric together, forming a cutting fold around your right thumb.

Shake the fabric free of wrinkles so that one smooth vertical fold descends to the bottom of the fabric. With your left hand, grasp the top edges near the vertical fold, making sure the top edges stay parallel.

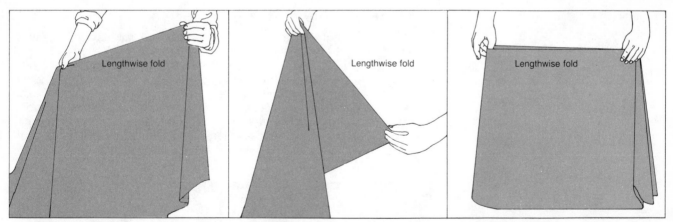

Grasp top edges of fabric, with right hand where cut will be.

Swing fabric around to bring top edges together with left hand.

Shake out wrinkles to form one fold at right hand.

Cutting on a flat surface. If you've decided to cut one stroke at a time, lay the fabric on a large table or the floor, holding the fold in place. Smooth the section to be cut back over the remaining fabric, and check to see that the lengthwise edges are aligned. Take your shears in one hand and place the other hand flat near the cutting fold to keep the fabric from slipping.

Vertical cutting with a single stroke. On many slipcover fabrics, you can start a cut along a vertical fold and just push the shears along, letting the grainline and gravity ease the job. The secret is in the proper use of the shears.

Insert the tip of the lower blade into the cutting fold (holding the fabric taut with the other hand). Start with the blades held apart at a 45-degree angle and push the lower blade in as far as it will go. With fabric held close to the body, cut the fabric slightly and *push*, keeping the blades open at a 30-degree angle. Experiment on similar fabric to find just the right angle and pressure.

No matter how hard you try, blades may open or fabric snag. Don't fret; simply start again. Cut slightly and push until you reach the fabric's opposite edge, where a snap of the blades severs remaining threads.

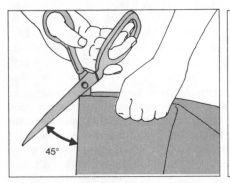

With shears open at a 45-degree angle, insert lower blade into cutting fold.

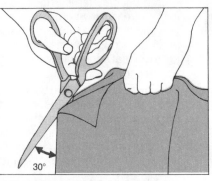

Keep blades open at a 30-degree angle as you push shears down.

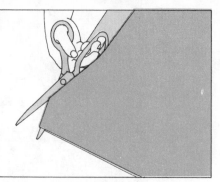

Finish the cut with a snap of the blades.

Sometimes in blocking out you'll need to make a rather long cut along the lengthwise grain of the fabric. Then you'll have to take two or more successive runs with your shears. Make sure your cutting fold parallels the fabric's edge. Once your first run ends (the length of your extended right arm), don't snap the blades shut. With your left hand, grasp the cut fabric edges just behind the open shears, cut slightly with your right hand, and continue to cut with blades open at a 30-degree angle.

Marking fabric sections

As you block out the various fabric sections, you will need to note what part of the chair or sofa they are for. Identify each section on a scrap of paper or on a piece of masking tape—you'll find abbreviations for most sections on the front-and-reverse drawings of the armchair. Applying the tape or pinning the identifying pieces of paper on the wrong side of each section will prevent positioning mistakes later. Pin the identified fabric sections in place wrong side out on the furniture as you go, roughly matching stripes or motifs if necessary. All scrap fabric should be set apart —you'll need some later for small parts of your slipcover.

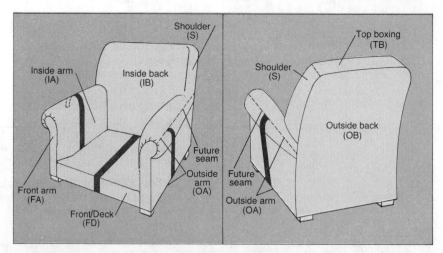

Using these section abbreviations, make masking tape or paper labels and attach them to the wrong sides of fabric sections.

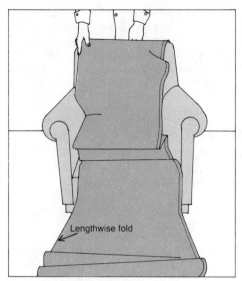

Fold fabric lengthwise and drape it down inside back and over deck.

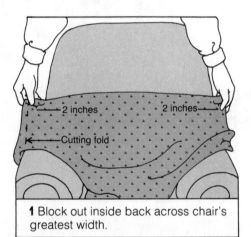

1 Block out inside back across chair's greatest width.

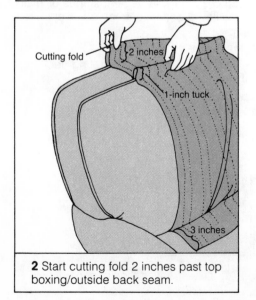

2 Start cutting fold 2 inches past top boxing/outside back seam.

Preparing to block out

Whether you plan to railroad your fabric or run it vertically up and over the furniture's arms and back, begin this way:

Remove all loose cushions.

Unroll the fabric and fold it in half lengthwise, if not already folded. You may fold the fabric either inside out or outside in, so long as you can see the pattern (if any) clearly enough to center or match motifs. Trim off selvages along both long edges of the fabric—selvages often pucker, distorting fabric's shape. It's especially important to trim selvages off for railroaded slipcovers so you can accurately allow for seam allowances along the bottom edges.

If you are using bedsheets, don't fold them in half lengthwise; instead, block out the widest part of your furniture (T-shaped deck, inside back that flares out) first and cut the entire sheet along that width. Use the remainder of this piece to block out other parts of the furniture.

Drape the fabric down the inside back and over the deck, letting it spill out in a cloth river across the floor. Position yourself, with measuring tape and shears, behind the piece of furniture. Start with the fold closest to your right hand.

Cutting instructions, both for railroading and for vertical run, assume that you know how to form a cutting fold and how to cut fabric (pages 53–54). Read through the entire blocking-out procedure before you begin; then be sure to follow steps in the sequence given, to avoid complications when centering and matching motifs.

If you're left-handed, use the hand opposite that named.

One last tip: As you drape fabric across upholstered sections, don't completely cover those sections. Leaving part of each section showing speeds the search for the best spot to start your cutting fold.

Step-by-step: Blocking out a fully upholstered armchair for railroaded fabric

You can railroad bedsheets as well as bolt fabrics, but most of the drawings that follow show bolt fabrics because most slipcovers are cut from these. Blocking-out techniques for railroading differ little for the various types of furniture. See pages 60–64 for technique variations.

1 **Inside back width.** Leaning over back of chair, grasp fold with right hand 3 feet from fabric's end. Swing fabric so that a 3-foot end lies horizontally across inside back, fold at top. Use left hand to place fabric's end at least 2 inches beyond back's greatest width—more if needed to center dominant motif.

Make cutting fold 2 inches past back's other side; cut.

2 **Inside back height.** Unfold section you just cut. Drape it, motifs showing, over chair's inside back. Center if printed with dominant motif, then raise fabric the height of missing deck cushion. For stripes or plaids, decide which major stripe or line you wish to place toward the bottom—this will affect positioning of other sections. Adjust bottom edge of fabric, allowing at least 3 inches to extend past crevice separating inside back and deck.

Stand at chair's side so that your right arm is nearest chair's back. At upholstery seam connecting top boxing to inside back, pinch a tuck (future slipcover seam) 1 inch high with left hand. (If you're not making top boxing, don't pinch tuck.) With right hand, start a cutting fold 2 inches past upholstery seam connecting top boxing to *outside* back; cut.

The larger piece comprises your top boxing and inside back. Identify it as TB/IB using the method described on page 54.

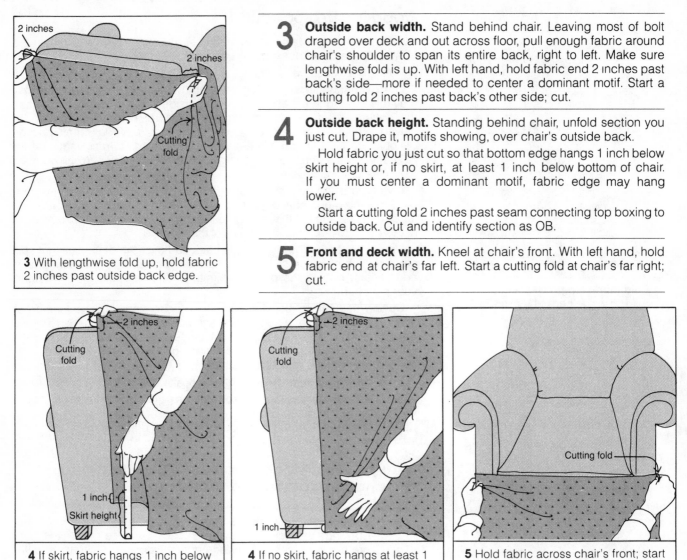

3 With lengthwise fold up, hold fabric 2 inches past outside back edge.

3 Outside back width. Stand behind chair. Leaving most of bolt draped over deck and out across floor, pull enough fabric around chair's shoulder to span its entire back, right to left. Make sure lengthwise fold is up. With left hand, hold fabric end 2 inches past back's side—more if needed to center a dominant motif. Start a cutting fold 2 inches past back's other side; cut.

4 Outside back height. Standing behind chair, unfold section you just cut. Drape it, motifs showing, over chair's outside back.

Hold fabric you just cut so that bottom edge hangs 1 inch below skirt height or, if no skirt, at least 1 inch below bottom of chair. If you must center a dominant motif, fabric edge may hang lower.

Start a cutting fold 2 inches past seam connecting top boxing to outside back. Cut and identify section as OB.

5 Front and deck width. Kneel at chair's front. With left hand, hold fabric end at chair's far left. Start a cutting fold at chair's far right; cut.

4 If skirt, fabric hangs 1 inch below skirt height.

4 If no skirt, fabric hangs at least 1 inch below chair bottom.

5 Hold fabric across chair's front; start cutting fold at right edge.

6 Front height, deck length. Unfold section you just cut and drape it, motifs showing, over chair's front and deck. If stripes or plaid, make sure that same stripe lies at bottom of front as lies at bottom of outside back.

See Step 4 to adjust for skirt or no skirt.

Start a cutting fold 3 inches past crevice separating deck from inside back; cut. Identify section as F/D.

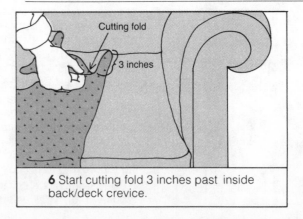

6 Start cutting fold 3 inches past inside back/deck crevice.

7 **Outside arm length.** Kneel at side of chair. Place fabric end at least 2 inches past chair's back edge, lengthwise fold at top. Center dominant motif (if any) between outside arm's front and rear. Form a cutting fold 2 inches past front of chair; cut.

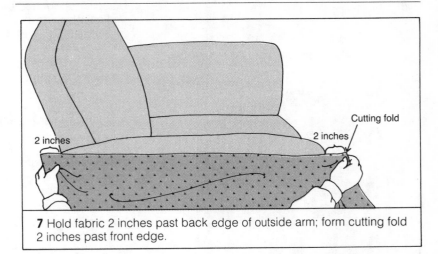

2 inches   2 inches   Cutting fold

7 Hold fabric 2 inches past back edge of outside arm; form cutting fold 2 inches past front edge.

8 **Outside arm height.** On upholstery, mark this future seam connecting outside arm with inside arm with blackboard chalk. Be sure to extend the line from front of arm to back of shoulder. (If chair arm slopes, see page 60.) For stripes or plaids, make sure bottom stripe or line on outside arm is the same as on front and outside back. Unfold section you just cut and drape it, motifs showing, over outside arm. If fabric has a dominant motif, center it between bottom of chair and future seam.

See Step 4 to adjust for skirt or no skirt.

With right hand, form a cutting fold 2 inches above future seam (dotted line in drawing); cut.

Identify section as OA; identify "scrap"—future inside arm— as IA.

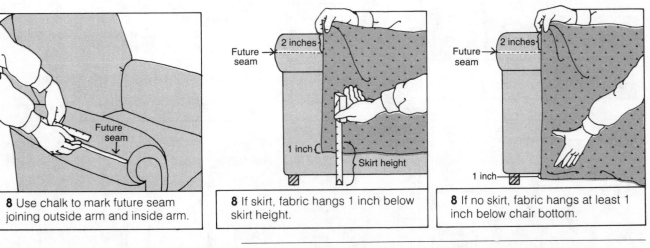

8 Use chalk to mark future seam joining outside arm and inside arm.

Future seam   2 inches   1 inch   Skirt height

8 If skirt, fabric hangs 1 inch below skirt height.

Future seam   2 inches   1 inch

8 If no skirt, fabric hangs at least 1 inch below chair bottom.

9 **Second outside arm.** Repeat Steps 7 and 8 on chair's other side.

You're through blocking out for now—you'll block out inside arm, front arm sections, and shoulder sections once you start pin-fitting (see page 65); after pin-fitting, you'll cut cushions and skirt (see page 80).

Step-by-step: Blocking out a fully upholstered armchair for vertically run fabric

Because of their motif or texture, some fabrics lend themselves to being draped vertically over the furniture's arms and back. Vertical blocking-out techniques differ somewhat from those used for railroading. They'll work with bolt fabrics and bedsheets, and on most furniture types. See pages 60–64 for technique variations.

Before you start, review "Preparing to block out" on page 55.

Note the direction of any pattern or pile (run your hand over velvet or corduroy to check). Arrange the fabric so that as you draw it up over the furniture, the pattern is upright and the pile runs downward.

1 **Inside back height.** Stand at chair's side so that your right arm is nearest chair's front. Drape fabric with fold toward you. With left hand, pull fabric end at least 2 inches past upholstery seam connecting top boxing to outside back.

Pull enough fabric up inside back so that, with right hand, you can pinch a tuck 1 inch high at upholstery seam connecting top boxing to *inside* back. (If you're not making top boxing, don't pinch tuck.) Center dominant motif (if any) between back's bottom and top, then raise motif the height of the missing deck cushion, adjusting tuck as needed.

Hold tuck secure with left hand. Form a cutting fold 3 inches past crevice separating inside back and deck; cut.

2 **Inside back width.** Stand behind chair and unfold fabric you just cut. Drape it, upright, over inside back.

With left hand, place fabric's edge at least 2 inches past edge of inside back at widest point—farther past if needed to center dominant motif. With right hand, form a cutting fold 2 inches beyond back's other side; cut.

The larger piece comprises top boxing and inside back. Identify it as TB/IB.

3 **Outside back height.** Kneel behind chair. Pull enough fabric up and over chair and down outside back so that edge hangs 1 inch below skirt height or, if no skirt, at least 1 inch below bottom of chair. If you must center a dominant motif, fabric edge may hang lower.

Form a cutting fold 2 inches past seam connecting top boxing to outside back; cut.

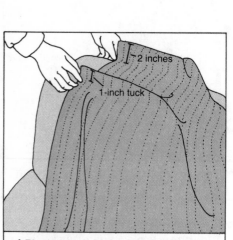

1 Pinch 1-inch-high tuck at seam connecting top boxing to inside back.

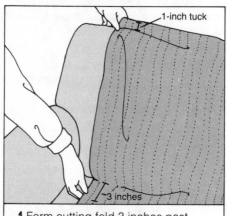

1 Form cutting fold 3 inches past inside back/deck crevice.

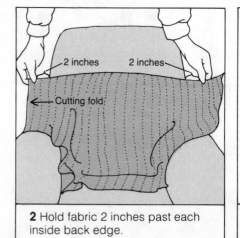

2 Hold fabric 2 inches past each inside back edge.

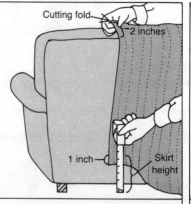

3 If skirt, fabric's edge hangs 1 inch below skirt height.

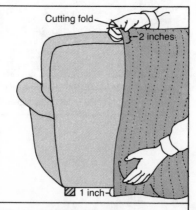

3 If no skirt, fabric hangs at least 1 inch below chair bottom.

4 **Outside back width.** Unfold fabric you just cut and drape it, upright, over outside back. With left hand, hold fabric at least 2 inches past edge of back at widest point—more than 2 inches if needed to center dominant motif.

Form a cutting fold 2 inches past back's other side; cut. Identify section as OB.

5 **Front height, deck length.** Kneel at side of chair closest to fabric's lengthwise fold. Place fabric end at least 3 inches above crevice separating deck from inside back. Raise end higher if you want to center a motif on chair's front.

Form a cutting fold 1 inch below skirt height or, if no skirt, at least 1 inch below bottom of chair; cut.

6 **Front and deck width.** Unfold fabric you just cut. Kneel in front of chair. With left hand, hold fabric edge at chair's far left. Form a cutting fold at chair's far right; cut. Identify section as F/D.

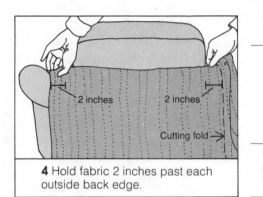

4 Hold fabric 2 inches past each outside back edge.

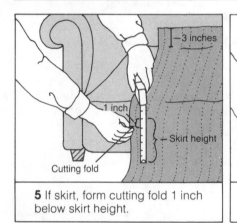

5 If skirt, form cutting fold 1 inch below skirt height.

5 If no skirt, form cutting fold at least 1 inch below chair bottom.

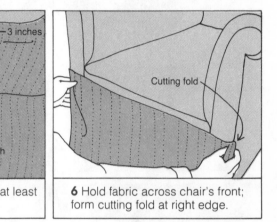

6 Hold fabric across chair's front; form cutting fold at right edge.

7 **Outside arm height.** On upholstery, mark with blackboard chalk future seam connecting inside arm with outside arm. Be sure to extend the line from front of arm to back of shoulder. (If chair arm slopes, see arm variations, page 60.) Stand at chair's side. Drape fabric with fold toward front. Pull fabric up inside and over arm so it hangs 1 inch below skirt height, or, if no skirt, at least 1 inch below bottom of chair. Center dominant motif (if any) between bottom of chair and future seam connecting outside with inside arm (dotted line in drawing), allowing extra fabric at bottom if necessary.

Form a cutting fold 2 inches above future seam (dotted line in drawing); cut.

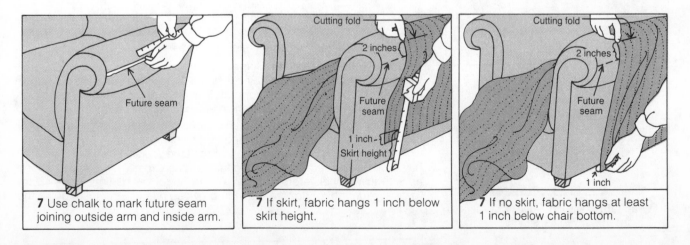

7 Use chalk to mark future seam joining outside arm and inside arm.

7 If skirt, fabric hangs 1 inch below skirt height.

7 If no skirt, fabric hangs at least 1 inch below chair bottom.

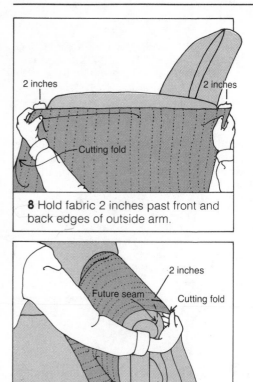

8 Hold fabric 2 inches past front and back edges of outside arm.

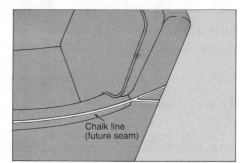

10 Form cutting fold 2 inches past outside arm/inside arm future seam.

On sloping arm, extend future seam chalk line to chair's back edge; if slope is extreme, level off chalk line.

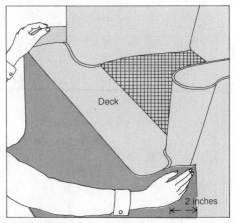

Wrap fabric around T-deck's corners 2 inches past vertical seams.

8 Outside arm length. Kneel at same side of chair as in Step 7. Unfold section you just cut and hold it upright. Hold fabric edge at least 2 inches past back edge of outside arm—more if needed to center dominant motif.

Form a cutting fold 2 inches past arm's front edge; cut. Identify section as OA.

9 Second outside arm. Repeat Steps 7 and 8 on chair's other side.

10 Inside arm height. Stand in front of chair. Pull enough fabric up outside arm and down inside arm so that fabric end is at least 3 inches beyond crevice separating inside arm and deck. Center dominant motif (if any) between crevice and top of arm, then raise it the height of the missing deck cushion (be sure to leave 3 inches of fabric overlapping crevice).

Form a cutting fold 2 inches past future seam connecting outside with inside arm (dotted line in drawing—same as in Step 7); cut. Identify section as IA.

11 Second inside arm height. Repeat Step 10.

You're through blocking out for now—you'll block out inside arm length, front arm sections, and shoulder sections once you start pin-fitting (see page 65); after pin-fitting, you'll cut cushions and skirt (see page 80).

Blocking-out variations

Though there are many different furniture types, blocking-out variations are few.

Arm variations. Some furniture arms don't have separate front arm sections. In such cases, while blocking out inside arm, extend fabric 2 inches past vertical upholstery seam at front of arm connecting inside and outside arm. If there is no upholstery seam, mark a vertical line with chalk for future seam.

Occasionally you'll encounter furniture arms that slope. When chalking a line for future seam separating inside from outside arm, be sure to continue angle of arm's slope all the way to back of chair. If that angle is extreme, level off chalk line where arm ends. When you block out outside arm, form cutting fold 2 inches above chalk line's highest point where it meets outside back.

Wings. More a design element than a blocking-out variation, wings can be thought of as large shoulder sections. Save blocking out of both inside and outside wings until you pin-fit back and deck. Like shoulder sections, wings can often be blocked out from scrap.

T-shaped deck. When blocking out front and deck width on a piece of furniture with T-shaped deck, wrap fabric around each corner of deck 2 inches past each vertical outside arm/deck seam.

Attached pillowback chair. Sometimes a back cushion looks as though it will come loose, but won't. Crevices on all three sides separate the edges of the cushion from its back support. This type of construction, called an attached pillowback, applies to chairs, love seats, and sofas.

The easiest way to slipcover such a piece is to ignore the crevices. You'll then need no complicated pinning at the corners, nor will you need to worry about the cover working loose each time you sit. Block out the inside back/top boxing section by pulling fabric tight across the crevice. Proceed as with fully upholstered armchair (page 55 for railroading; page 58 for vertically run fabric). Ignore the side crevices by blocking them out in the

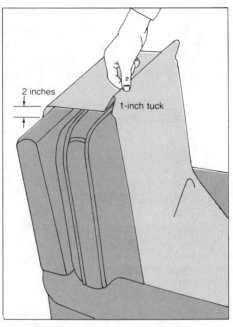

Simplify the slipcover on an attached pillowback by ignoring the crevices.

same way you block out shoulders during pin-fitting (page 69). Before slipping on the finished cover, you can stuff top and side crevices with cotton or polyester batting to minimize sagging.

Barrelback chair. With a piece of blackboard chalk, divide both inside back and outside back into three equal vertical sections (see drawing). The chalk lines mark future seams. Treat the middle section as inside and outside back, the two flanking sections as inside and outside arms. If inside back is deeply curved, you may have to further divide middle section into three sections. Depending on depth of curve, the three sections may equal, or the two side sections (closest to inside arms) may be smaller. Before blocking out, chalk lines for future seams. Proceed as for the fully upholstered armchair (starting on page 55).

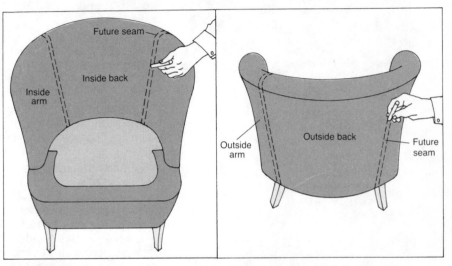

Use chalk to divide a barrelback chair's inside back and outside back into three equal vertical sections.

Channeled furniture. Channels are the vertical grooves splitting the inside back of a piece of furniture into tapering segments. You'll find channels on many types of furniture.

You can make your job easier by ignoring the channels. Before blocking out, pad inside back with a single layer of polyester batting, secured on top and sides by whipstitching (see drawing) and at bottom by tucking in. Trim batting around top and side edges if necessary; leave 3 inches for bottom tuck-in.

Polyester batting is usually available at fabric stores in a 54-inch width; this width is enough to run batting vertically on most chairs. To determine yardage needed, measure inside back of chair at highest point and add 6 inches for tucking in at deck and wrapping over top. For love seats, sofas, and sofabeds, you must railroad batting. To determine yardage needed, measure inside back across its greatest width and add 6 inches for wrapping around sides.

If your channeled furniture is also a barrelback, batting stretched around the curves will smooth out the scalloped effect. Anchor batting at center back with T-pins. Working toward front on each side, gently stretch batting around barrelback, anchoring as you go. Start whipstitching on one side where inside arm meets deck; work up and all the way around to other side of chair. Trim batting along future seam between inside/outside back and arms; leave 3 inches for bottom tuck-in.

To divide inside and outside back into three vertical sections, see "Barrelback chair," above. Further dividing inside back into sections that duplicate upholstery channels will give a smooth fit around the curve. Mark vertical lines on batting where inside back channels lie underneath; use these lines as guides to block out inside back sections. Proceed as for fully upholstered armchair (starting on page 55).

Batting whipstitched to inside back and arms smooths out channels.

Blocking out love seats, sofas, sofabeds

Once you've solved a few problems relating to the inside back, the outside back, and the front/deck, slipcovering wide furniture becomes as simple as slipcovering a chair. Though a sofabed requires some special steps at the pin-fitting and sewing stages, it is blocked out like a love seat or sofa of the same width. If your sofabed has a T-shaped deck, block out deck the width of the "T."

The problems of blocking out wide furniture concern motif centering and symmetry. You deal with them in different ways, depending on whether you plan to railroad fabric or run it vertically.

Railroaded. The easy way to railroad the inside back on wide furniture is to ignore vertical welt, channels (see page 61), or attached back pillows (page 60) and follow instructions for the fully upholstered armchair that begin on page 55.

If the slipcover's inside back will have unwelted seams, you may want to slash the upholstered welt along its spine with a razor blade, then pull the cording free and cut it off at its bottom and top. This prevents the slipcover from wearing excessively over upholstery welt; of course it also makes the furniture look tattered without a slipcover.

If you wish to duplicate upholstered vertical welt, pinch or allow for an extra 1-inch-high tuck wherever welt occurs. You will cut these tucks for seams during pin-fitting—but leave the blocked-out inside back intact for now.

Suppose the inside back of your wide furniture is "tight"—with neither loose cushions nor attached pillows. Suppose, further, that your fabric has a dominant motif which you've decided you want to center on each deck cushion. To line up a dominant motif on the inside back with each deck cushion, you may have to divide the back fabric vertically into cushion-wide sections (add 1-inch seam allowances). But first try shifting the fabric back and forth across the inside back to see if you can be satisfied to have motifs out of line with the cushions but symmetrically placed between the back's left and right sides.

Ease blocking out by railroading inside back as one piece.

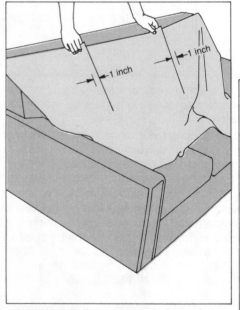

To duplicate vertical upholstery welt, allow 1-inch-high tucks.

On wide furniture with no separate back cushions, try placing motifs out of line with deck cushions but symmetrically between left and right sides.

To allow for the tops and far left and right sides of attached pillows, follow instructions for the attached pillowback chair (page 60), ignoring the crevices.

The vertical grooves *between* attached pillows (as narrow as channels, but deeper), are also best ignored. Pinch or allow for a 1-inch-high tuck for each groove, cutting later during pin-fitting (or now if you need much extra fabric for centering).

Vertically run. Two widths of fabric 45 or more inches wide usually will cover the back of a love seat, sofa, or sofabed up to 7½ feet wide. If you simply want to sew weltless vertical seams connecting the two widths over the inside back, the outside back, and the front/deck, follow instructions for a fully upholstered armchair (starting on page 55), cutting a second piece for each of these wide sections.

When you block out wide furniture for height, make sure you cut each fabric piece at the same point in the design scheme, so that what shows at the furniture's top right also shows at its top left, on the inside back, outside back, and front/deck. When you block out furniture for width, obtain symmetry by positioning motifs the same distance from the furniture's right and left edges.

Two widths of 45-inch-wide fabric vertically run will cover the backs of most sofas and sofabeds.

On inside back, make sure you center motifs between top and bottom as well as left and right.

To line up dominant motifs with deck cushions or to allow for attached back pillows, refer to "Railroaded," page 62.

Blocking out an ottoman

If you're covering an oblong ottoman to match a chair, block out the ottoman last, with the chair's front/deck section in place. Center the ottoman in front of the chair.

You block out ottomans, whether square, oblong, or round, in the same five steps.

• *Step 1: Top.* If ottoman is oblong, first block out in same direction that motif runs on chair's deck; if ottoman is square or round, direction of chair fabric makes no difference. Place fabric, folded lengthwise, across top so it extends at least 2 inches past each side. Allow more fabric if needed to center dominant motif. Make cutting fold; cut.

• *Step 2: Top.* Unfold fabric. Position at least 2 inches past other two sides (or, if ottoman is round, 2 inches plus diameter plus 2 inches). Make cutting fold; cut. Identify section as OT (ottoman top).

If ottoman is round, divide circumference into four equal segments. Mark future vertical seams (dotted lines in drawing) on upholstery with chalk.

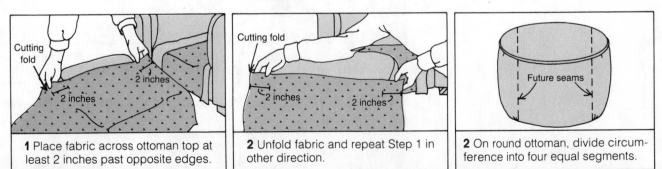

1 Place fabric across ottoman top at least 2 inches past opposite edges.

2 Unfold fabric and repeat Step 1 in other direction.

2 On round ottoman, divide circumference into four equal segments.

Railroaded. If matching chair's deck motifs run arm to arm, follow Steps 3–5 that follow.

- *Step 3: Sides' width.* Place fabric folded lengthwise along side's longest dimension (¼ of round ottoman's circumference), 2 inches past each corner (past round ottoman's two adjacent chalked vertical seams). Make cutting fold; cut.

- *Step 4: Sides' height.* Unfold fabric and hold it so bottom edge hangs 1 inch below skirt height or, if no skirt, at least 1 inch below ottoman's bottom. Make cutting fold 2 inches above ottoman's top; cut.

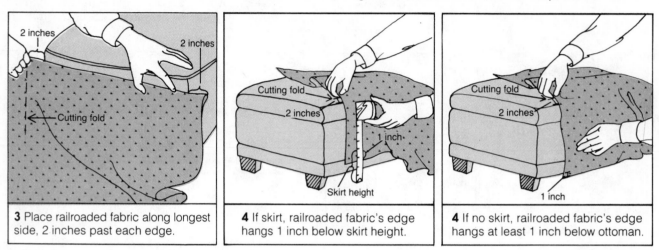

3 Place railroaded fabric along longest side, 2 inches past each edge.

4 If skirt, railroaded fabric's edge hangs 1 inch below skirt height.

4 If no skirt, railroaded fabric's edge hangs at least 1 inch below ottoman.

- *Step 5: Remaining sides.* Repeat Steps 3 and 4 for each of the three remaining sides.

Vertically run. If matching chair's deck motifs run front to back, follow Steps 3–5 that follow.

- *Step 3: Sides' height.* Hold folded fabric so bottom edge hangs 1 inch below skirt height or, if no skirt, at least 1 inch below ottoman's bottom. Make cutting fold 2 inches above ottoman's top; cut.

- *Step 4: Sides' width.* Unfold fabric and hold along side's longest dimension (¼ of round ottoman's circumference), 2 inches past each corner (past round ottoman's two adjacent chalked vertical seams). Make cutting fold; cut.

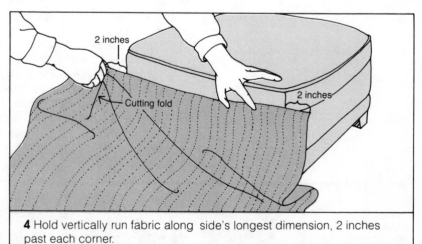

4 Hold vertically run fabric along side's longest dimension, 2 inches past each corner.

- *Step 5: Remaining sides.* Repeat Steps 3 and 4 for each of the three remaining sides.

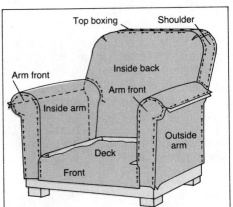

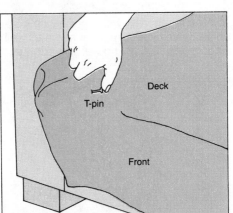

Pin-fitting

Pin-fitting is the process of joining blocked-out fabric sections before sewing them together. By pinning sections together directly on your chair or sofa, you get a snug, individualized fit.

You'll find that the techniques we offer will alter the structural look of your furniture in places—shoulders will extend farther down, front arm sections may appear to be wider. We recommend these changes to simplify both the construction of your slipcover and the lines of your furniture. Interestingly, the fewer upholstered surface details a slipcover attempts to duplicate, the more it will resemble upholstery.

Most slipcovers can be pin-fitted wrong side out, saving you considerable time and effort. With wrong-side pin-fitting, you needn't notch all seams, remove pins (125 to 150 for a fully upholstered armchair), turn the fabric inside out, and repin seams before sewing. On most slipcover fabrics, the pattern shows through clearly enough on the wrong side to allow you to center and match motifs. And since most furniture is symmetrical, you can count on your cover to fit (perhaps with minor adjustments) when it is turned right side out.

But if your fabric's pattern doesn't show through, you'll have to pin it together with right sides showing in order to center and match motifs. And if you're covering asymmetric furniture, such as a one-arm sectional, you can't pin-fit it wrong side out—the slipcover's arm would be at the opposite end of the sectional when the cover was turned right side out. Pages 79–80 give details on right-side-out pin-fitting.

Whether your fabric is railroaded or vertically run, the pin-fitting method is the same—just place each fabric section with its marked side up. Skirted and skirtless slipcovers are pin-fitted alike; you'll chalk or adjust outside sections for skirt height or lower edge as you anchor them to the furniture.

In addition to the essentials—shears, chalk, T-pins, and a box of 1 1/16-inch dressmaking pins—you'll find a lightweight 12-inch ruler helpful. Less bulky but more rigid than a steel measuring tape, it is handy for setting skirt height from the floor and for tucking fabric into crevices. A ruler also will disclose variations in the furniture's structural symmetry, such as in the width of its arms (page 73 tells you how to compensate for differences of 1/2 inch or less).

Whether you pin-fit fabric wrong or right side out, you'll use the following basic techniques throughout.

Anchor-pinning

Anchor pins act as extra hands to hold fabric sections in place while you pin them together. Once you've positioned a section on the furniture, smooth the fabric over the upholstery, working from the center toward one edge and then the other. Make sure you square the fabric's pattern with the lines of the furniture. Fix T-pins in two adjacent corners, pull fabric gently taut, and anchor the remaining two corners. Sometimes you'll have to remove the first two pins, adjust the fabric, then put them back in. On larger sections, additional anchor pins around the perimeter will help keep the fabric straight and smooth.

To ensure that each anchor pin holds, drive the point at a 45-degree angle toward the outer edge of the fabric until it penetrates the upholstery. Then push the pin *head* toward the outer edge, pivoting the shank, and drive the point all the way in. Slanting away from the edge toward the section's center, the pin will hold the fabric tight.

Positioning & marking lower edge

As you anchor fabric pieces to the outside back, front/deck, outside arms, and (possibly) front arms, you'll have to determine where the lower edge

Pin-fitting a slipcover wrong side out will save you work.

First push point of anchor pin toward outer edge, barely piercing upholstery.

Push pin head toward outer edge; then drive point in toward center.

should fall. For unpatterned fabrics that don't need to be shifted or matched, anchor the section with the bottom edge 1 inch below the future skirt height, or for a skirtless cover, 1 inch below the chair bottom.

If matching or centering patterns leaves excess fabric below, chalk a horizontal dotted line (for trimming later) 1 inch below future skirt height or the chair's bottom edge.

Pin-basting

Pin-basting is the method we recommend for joining fabric sections along future seams, whether the seams are meant to result in loose folds (as with tuck-ins) or to fit snugly against upholstered seams.

In most cases you start pin-basting at the center of the future seam and work toward the ends; the pins actually form the seamline. Each pin should penetrate both layers of slipcover fabric without entering the upholstery, and it should re-emerge ½ inch away; place pins approximately 1 inch apart. Facing all the pins in the same direction minimizes pricked fingers and speeds pins' removal when you begin to sew.

Pinning a seamline. Here's how to pin-baste a snug-fitting seamline.

- *Step 1:* Anchor-pin two adjacent fabric sections onto furniture.
- *Step 2:* Hold fabric edges between middle finger and thumb of left hand close to spot you plan to pin.
- *Step 3:* Slide finger back and forth over thumb to pull both sections gently taut and cinch fabric up against upholstery welt (or weltless seam).
- *Step 4:* Holding fabric taut, pin flaps together with right hand. If upholstery seam is welted and you plan to welt your slipcover seam as well, pin to one side of upholstery welt, not on top. Welt riding welt is wobbly and gives seams a top-heavy look.

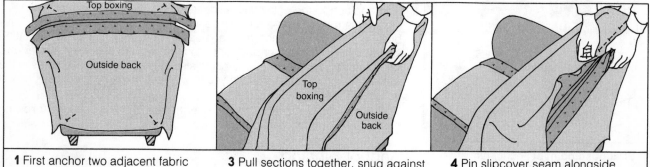

1 First anchor two adjacent fabric sections onto furniture.

3 Pull sections together, snug against upholstery welt or seam.

4 Pin slipcover seam alongside upholstery welt, not on top.

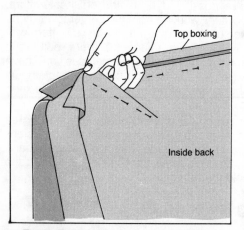

Form dart by pinching excess fabric together against upholstery; pin.

Trimming off scrap. Make it a rule to trim off waste in stages—a little at a time. You can always trim off more, but you can't sew it back on.

As you progress with your pin-fitting, you'll want to keep the fabric trimmed so that, when you finish, most pinned seams will have ½-inch allowances (unless otherwise specified). Pin one seam completely before you trim, then move on to the next. You'll do considerable trimming, especially when you're working with fabric that must fit around curves. Never trim where you haven't pinned.

Making darts. Darts allow fabric to conform to furniture's curves. You make a dart by pinching excess fabric together and cinching it against the upholstery with one or more pins. You then trim the flap of fabric to within ½ inch of the pins. Later a seam replaces the pins.

Slitting. Sometimes you must ease two fabric sections around the seam curve before pin-basting them together (for example, where the back flares over the arms or where a T-deck curves around set-back arms). Slitting each section's outer edge, usually to within 1 inch of the curved junction between two sections, releases tension in the fabric and lets it hug the upholstery without puckering while you pin. The longer the curve, the more slits you need to make.

Step-by-step: Pin-fitting a fully upholstered armchair

The steps that follow include instructions for trimming seams and blocking out the remaining fabric sections, since these operations intertwine with the pin-fitting itself. You start with the front/deck section (not the inside back, as in blocking out). *Even if you're slipcovering another type of furniture such as a sofa, wing chair, barrelback chair, sofabed or ottoman, it's essential to read through these armchair instructions.* With the exception of the ottoman (see page 78), variations on pin-fitting are based on these techniques.

Before you start, find out whether or not your furniture is symmetrical within a half-inch—back the same height on the right as on the left, arms the same width. Symmetry allows you to pin-fit fabric wrong side out; page 69 shows how to adjust a pin-fitted cover for symmetry variations of a half-inch or less in arms. For asymmetric furniture, see page 79.

1 **Determine skirt height.** (If you don't plan to add a skirt, begin with step 2.) Height of skirt will depend on personal preference and on your furniture's proportions and design. If you are covering an upholstered skirt, make sure slipcover skirt hides it completely. On furniture with no skirt now, measure from floor to height you want slipcover skirt to reach. (Skirts are typically 6 inches high, but can go to 10 or more inches for certain boudoir and wing chairs.)

Once you have determined skirt's finished height, write the measurement down, because you'll need it later when you cut skirt out.

In steps 2, 3, 11, and 28 following, anchor slipcover sections 1 inch *below* finished skirt height. This provides for a ½-inch seam to join skirt to slipcover, plus an extra ½ inch to allow for slight hiking up that can occur when anchor pins are removed.

2 **Anchor front/deck.** Smooth fabric over front and deck, allowing at least 3 inches to extend past crevice at inside back and at each inside arm. Anchor at front of deck, then fold tuck-in flaps back from crevices so section lies flat on deck. Chalk trim line, if needed, for skirt or bottom edge.

For deck variations, see page 74.

3 **Anchor outside back.** Anchor section, allowing at least 2 inches to hang past outside back top, and centering any dominant motif. If you're working with horizontal stripes, match outside back to front by placing the back piece so that a specific stripe is the same distance up from chair's bottom edge on the back as on the front. Then, outside arm and front arm can match outside back and front. Chalk trim line, if needed, for skirt or bottom edge.

4 **Anchor inside back/top boxing.** Center any dominant motif, then raise it the height of missing deck cushion. Smooth fabric so that at least 3 inches falls past deck crevice (for tuck-in) and at least 4 inches hangs past top boxing down outside back. Anchor section in place.

For inside back variations, see pages 74–75.

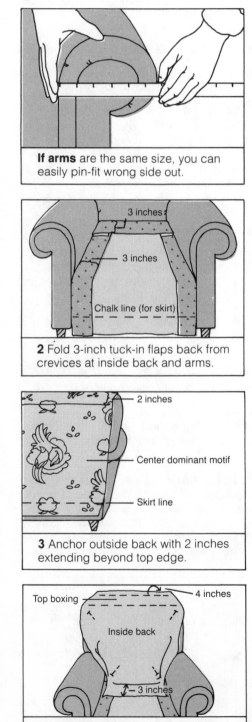

If arms are the same size, you can easily pin-fit wrong side out.

2 Fold 3-inch tuck-in flaps back from crevices at inside back and arms.

3 Anchor outside back with 2 inches extending beyond top edge.

4 Four inches should extend past back edge of top boxing.

5 **Slit upper inside back seam allowance.** With finger tips, push fabric fold against—but not into—crevice that separates inside back from arm. To allow fabric to fit smoothly, you must slit upper part of flap.

Start your first (and longest) cut two-thirds of the way up between deck and top of arm, where inside back begins to flare outward. Snip in a slight upward direction to within 1 inch of crevice. Make two more cuts, starting each from the upper edge of preceding cut, ending the series on a level with top of arm. Cut off excess below slits to within 3 inches of crevice.

Repeat with other side of inside back.

If pin-fitting a barrelback chair, postpone this step until Step 23.

6 **Baste inside back to deck.** Make sure inside back tuck-in flap lies on top of deck tuck-in flap. Pin-baste flaps together 2½ inches from crevice.

7 **Anchor top boxing.** Pinch a tuck 1 inch high at upholstery seam that connects inside back to top boxing. Smooth fabric over top boxing. Anchor boxing with one pin 1 inch from where top boxing and shoulder meet on one side, pull fabric taut, and anchor at chair's other side.

If furniture has no top boxing, pin-baste inside back directly to outside back.

For attached pillowback variations, see page 75.

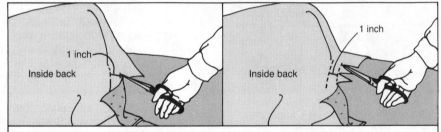

5 Make first inside back slit two-thirds of the way up; last slit should be on a level with top of arm.

8 **Pin-baste inside back/top boxing tuck.** Stand at side of chair. Pin-baste tuck snugly, following welted seam and pinning along side of welt nearest outside back.

9 **Pin-baste outside back to top boxing.** Stand at back of chair. Pin-baste outside back to top boxing along lower side of welted upholstery seam. Inside back tuck and outside back/top boxing seam should be parallel. If chair is old, upholstery seams may have bulged out of line; if so, correct tuck by removing center pins, replacing them to form a straight line with left and right outermost pins.

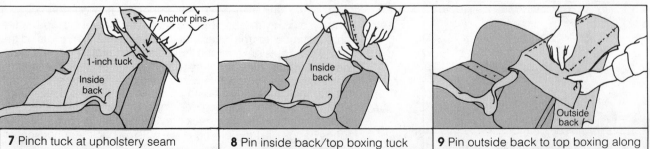

7 Pinch tuck at upholstery seam connecting inside back to top boxing.

8 Pin inside back/top boxing tuck along upholstery seam.

9 Pin outside back to top boxing along lower side of upholstery seam.

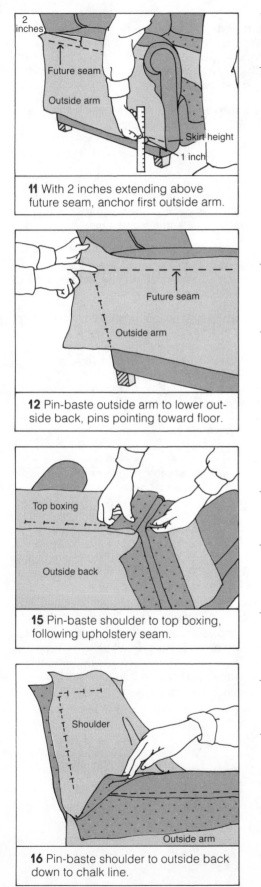

11 With 2 inches extending above future seam, anchor first outside arm.

12 Pin-baste outside arm to lower outside back, pins pointing toward floor.

15 Pin-baste shoulder to top boxing, following upholstery seam.

16 Pin-baste shoulder to outside back down to chalk line.

10 **Trim top boxing.** Trim tuck that connects top boxing to inside back, creating ½-inch seam allowance. Trim top boxing/outside back seam allowance to ½ inch.

11 **Anchor first outside arm.** With tape measure or ruler, measure each front arm section at its widest point. If one arm is wider (by up to ½ inch) pin-fit that arm first. When you get to the second arm, pin-fit its front section to the same width as first arm. Then, when you turn the cover right side out, you can easily take in the slack for narrower arm by following the steps outlined on page 73. Taking in slack is much simpler than trying to expand seams, once you've trimmed their allowances to ½ inch.

Center any dominant motif or match horizontal stripes with outside back. Allow at least 2 inches of fabric above future seam (chalked on upholstery during blocking-out process) that separates outside from inside arm. Anchor fabric, then chalk trim line, if needed, for skirt or bottom edge.

12 **Pin-baste outside arm to lower outside back.** Pins pointing toward floor, pin from center of section to bottom of chair, then up from center to chalk line on upholstery (future seam) that divides outside from inside arm.

13 **Shape first shoulder.** For construction ease, bottom of slipcover shoulder may ride above or extend below upholstered shoulder to chalk line that divides outside from inside arm. Cut a piece of scrap at least 4 inches wider than widest part of upholstered shoulder and at least 4 inches longer than *slipcover* shoulder's height. If you are working with horizontal stripes, try to match them to either the inside or outside back before you cut (trying to match them to both usually proves futile).

For furniture with wings, substitute the words "outside wing" for "shoulder" in Steps 13, 14, 15 (if top boxing), 16, 19, and 20.

14 **Anchor shoulder.** Anchor shoulder top, pull fabric taut, then anchor bottom just above chalk line on upholstery that divides outside from inside arm.

15 **Pin-baste shoulder to top boxing.** Begin pin-basting at point where shoulder and upholstered top boxing meet. Place pins 1 inch apart, starting at outside back, stopping at corner of inside back.

16 **Pin-baste shoulder to outside back.** Starting at center of seam, pin-baste up to top of shoulder, down to chalk line that divides outside from inside arm. If upholstery is welted, pin along welt's outside back side.

17 **Pin-baste shoulder to inside back.** Starting at center of seam, pin-baste up to top of shoulder, down to top of arm. If upholstery is welted, pin along welt's shoulder side.

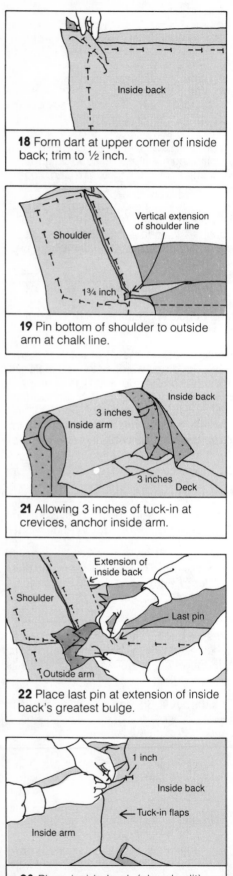

18 Form dart at upper corner of inside back; trim to ½ inch.

19 Pin bottom of shoulder to outside arm at chalk line.

21 Allowing 3 inches of tuck-in at crevices, anchor inside arm.

22 Place last pin at extension of inside back's greatest bulge.

23 Place inside back (already slit) over unslit upper inside arm.

18 **Close top corner with dart.** To help fabric hug chair's form, you may need a dart at upper corner of inside back where top boxing, shoulder, and inside back meet. Pin any excess fabric into a dart, and trim dart seam allowance to ½ inch. Trim seam allowances of top boxing/shoulder and inside back/shoulder to ½ inch.

19 **Pin-baste shoulder to outside arm.** Starting at outside back and keeping pins parallel to floor, use three pins to baste bottom of shoulder to outside arm at chalk line. Point of last pin should emerge 1¾ inches behind vertical extension of shoulder's forward line.

Pinch together flaps from bottom of shoulder and top of outside arm. Cut straight in on imaginary line toward point where last pin emerges, but stop ½ inch short of chair. Pivot shears toward outside back so blades parallel pins, and trim remaining seam allowance to ½ inch.

20 **Trim shoulder/outside back/outside arm.** Starting at top of shoulder, trim seam allowance to ½ inch. Continue to trim down through shoulder/outside back and outside arm/outside back.

21 **Anchor inside arm.** If fabric has a dominant motif, center it on inside arm, then raise it the height of missing deck cushion. If there are stripes, match them to inside back (railroaded) or outside arm (vertically run). As you position fabric, allow at least 3 inches of tuck-in where inside arm meets inside back, and at least 3 inches where inside arm meets deck. Top edge should come at least 2 inches past chalk line on upholstery that divides inside arm from outside arm. Anchor fabric. Trim tuck-ins to 3 inches if necessary.

For arm top variations, see page 76.

22 **Pin-baste inside arm to outside arm.** Work from center to front of arm, then to extension of inside back at its greatest bulge.

If arm has top boxing, pin-baste it to outside arm, then to inside arm.

23 **Slit upper inside arm.** Make sure inside back seam allowance (slit in step 5) lies on top of unslit inside arm seam allowance, and that the folds of both lie as snugly as possible against (but not in) the crevice separating inside back from inside arm.

Pinching both flaps together, slit inside arm, duplicating slits made on inside back. Cut no closer to crevice than 1 inch.

Baste tops of tuck-in below bottom slit with a single pin at a 45-degree angle. No further pinning is needed on tuck-in. Flap edges naturally fit together when you start sewing; since edges will be hidden, the tuck-in seam need not be perfectly straight.

For arm/inside back variations, see page 76.

If pin-fitting a barrelback chair, combine Step 5 with this step so you are slitting inside arm and inside back seam allowances at the same time, starting two-thirds of the way up from deck to chair's top.

24 **Baste inside arm to inside back/shoulder.** Starting at lowest slit, snugly pin-baste slit seam allowances against (but not in) upper crevice, to point where upholstered shoulder connects with inside back. Trim seam allowance to ½ inch, stopping where top pin *emerges* (not where point ends). Snip off waste.

Pin-baste last of inside arm to bottom of shoulder—you'll probably need only two pins. Trim remaining seam allowance to ½ inch.

25 **Finish basting inside arm to outside arm.** Use one or two pins to continue future inside arm/outside arm seam until it abuts seam that joins bottom of shoulder to outside arm.

Starting at front of arm, trim entire inside arm/outside arm seam allowance to ½ inch.

26 **Pin-baste tuck-in between front of inside arm and front/deck.** Like armchair shown, many pieces of furniture have a "spring-edge" deck, which springs independently up and down at arm's front rather than being connected with the arm at arm's front. A special tuck-in allowance between inside arm and deck at deck's front corner provides "give" when you sit; otherwise slipcover seam would rip.

To shape the tuck-in for a spring-edge deck, hold inside arm and deck pieces together and place a single basting pin parallel to and 2 inches from inside arm/deck crevice at front of chair. Snip curved wedge from pinned tuck-in, leaving ½-inch seam allowance near pin.

Push pinned tuck-in into crevice at front of chair. Rest of tuck-in, extending to inside back, need not be pinned.

For arm/deck variations, see pages 76–77. For sofabeds, see page 78.

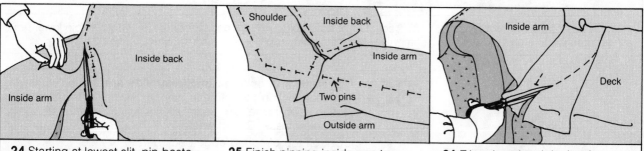

24 Starting at lowest slit, pin-baste inside arm to inside back/shoulder.

25 Finish pinning inside arm to outside arm with one or two pins.

26 Trim pinned tuck-in, leaving ½-inch allowance near pin.

27 On spring-edge deck, pin corner dart from front and side fabric.

27 **Pin dart at front corner of spring edge.** This step applies only to full-arm, spring-edge deck. Pinch together fabric from front of deck and side of deck at corner and secure with a single pin.

28 **Shape and anchor first front arm section.** Cut a piece of scrap 4 inches wider than front arm's greatest width. Anchor fabric to front arm with at least 2 inches extending beyond top of arm (trim to 2 inches if necessary). Chalk trimline, if needed, for skirt or bottom edge.

If fabric is striped, match front arm and deck front sections. If outside back and deck front pieces were positioned carefully with horizontal stripes matching and if outside arm was matched to outside back, front arm should now match outside arm. Such precise matching is difficult; if all pieces don't line up, be content with matching deck front and front arm sections.

For arm front variations, see page 77.

29

Pin-baste front arm section to inside/outside arm. Drawing shows upholstered (smaller) and slipcover (larger) contour of front arm section. At top of slipcover contour, connect front arm section to inside arm section with single pin.

Start halfway down inside arm edge and pin-baste to 1 inch below deck, then up to the pin at top of front arm section. Make a dart where inside arm starts to curve toward top, if needed.

Positioning your next pin is crucial for ensuring a snug slipcover fit. Starting at a point no more than ½ inch beneath arm's undercurl, and pinning as close as possible to upholstery welt, baste lower part of front arm section to outside arm (point pins downward). Continue pin-basting vertically, following upholstery welt to bottom of arm section.

Starting at pin inserted beneath arm's undercurl, pin-baste up to the pin at top of front arm section.

Pin-baste vertical edge of deck front to lower vertical edge of front arm section.

On a no-spring-edge T-deck, pin lower outside arm to side of deck front.

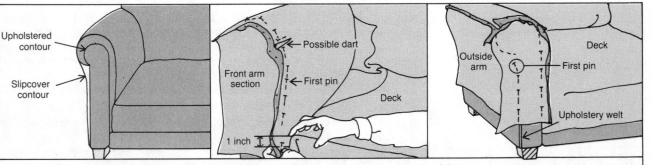

29 Slipcover contour is larger than upholstered contour on front arm.

29 Begin pin-basting front arm section halfway down inside arm edge.

29 At arm's undercurl, pin lower front arm section to outside arm.

30

Trim front arm section, inside/outside arm. If you've made a dart near section's top, trim to ½ inch. Starting at top of front arm section, trim inside arm seam allowance to ½ inch, stopping 1 inch below deck. Cut off waste.

Cut off top of spring-edge-deck dart to ½ inch.

Continuing down from point 1 inch below deck, pinching both fabric flaps together, trim seam allowance to ½ inch.

Free the fabric at arm's undercurl by cutting into it to within ½ inch of pins. Return to top of front arm section and trim outside arm seam allowance to bottom.

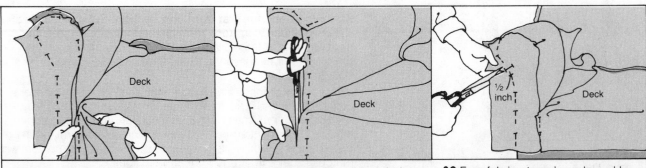

29 Pin vertical edges of deck and lower front arm section.

30 Pinch flaps together 1 inch below deck; trim allowance to ½ inch.

30 Free fabric at arm's undercurl by cutting to within ½ inch of pins.

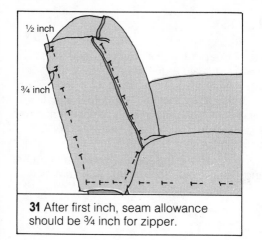

31 After first inch, seam allowance should be ¾ inch for zipper.

31 Repeat steps 11 through 30 on opposite side of chair, with two exceptions.

Exception for step 20 (Trim shoulder/outside back/outside arm): Your slipcover needs a zipper so that you can easily put the cover on and take it off. On opposite side of chair, starting at top, trim outside back seam allowance to ½ inch for the first inch only. Then taper out to ¾ inch, maintaining a ¾-inch zipper allowance all the way down outside back.

A slipcover zipper starts 1 inch from the furniture's top and extends to the bottom of the slipcover or skirt. Because you'll have to remove zipper-allowance pins to get slipcover off, chalk the line they form (on outside back piece); chalk line will help you repin the seam or press under seam allowances.

You'll need a zipper the proper length. If your cover will have a skirt, you'll need a zipper equal to finished measurement of outside back and skirt, plus ½ inch. If no skirt, add 3½ inches to slipcover outside back height. Upholstery supply stores and some fabric shops carry continuous zippers on rolls; you pay by the inch. Or you can buy a standard-length zipper (36, 45, and 54 inches are common) and snip off the excess.

Exception for step 30 (Baste front arm section to inside/outside arm). Remembering that final cover will be reversed, pin-baste second front arm section the same width as first, even if second arm is slightly narrower than first. You can take in excess later, but you can't easily let out the seam once you've trimmed allowance to ½ inch.

Making sure the slipcover fits

Before sewing the slipcover, you'll want to make sure the cover fits snugly right side out. Take time to chalk pinned lines along slit curves and critical corners, in case a few pins fall out when you turn the slipcover right side out. Remove anchor pins and basting pins (except top basting pin) from zipper allowance and carefully peel basted cover off chair.

Reverse the cover and place it on the chair right side out. If the cover looks too loose in spots, here's how to improve the fit:

- *Step 1:* Reaching through seam, pluck offending pins out.
- *Step 2:* Pull loosened seam allowance out through gap.
- *Step 3:* Repin on outside; retrim seam allowance to ½ inch.
- *Step 4:* Remove pins placed in Step 3. (Later, when you turn cover wrong side out again for sewing, you needn't bother replacing adjustment pins; since you removed only two or three of them, your seamline will hold.)
- *Step 5:* While slipcover is on chair, check and trim length around bottom edges. If adding a skirt, bottom edge should be ½ inch lower than finished skirt height. Remove cover and trim excess. If no skirt, fabric should hang 1 inch below bottom of chair.

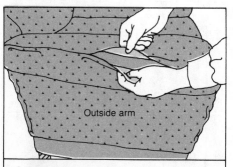

2 With cover right side out, pull out loosened seam allowances.

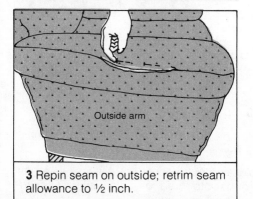

3 Repin seam on outside; retrim seam allowance to ½ inch.

Pin-fitting Variations

Pin-fitting fabric to furniture is a lot like pin-fitting clothes to people—whatever the variations, the purpose is to obtain a good fit.

This section first covers wrong-side-out pin-fitting variations that occur on different parts of furniture—deck, back, and arms. Then other variations, such as pin-fitting an ottoman and right-side-out pin-fitting on asymmetrical furniture, are dealt with. Though you will read about each variation separately, you may find that your furniture piece has several of them.

Before you begin any pin-fitting variations, reread the basic techniques for anchor-pinning, pin-basting, making darts, slitting, and trimming—pages 65–67.

Deck variations

Two common deck variations are the curved deck (found on a *chaise longue,* for example) and the T-shaped deck (common to many types of furniture).

If the front of your deck curves outward (or, more rarely, inward), you need to cut a separate piece for front boxing. Leave 1 inch below skirt height or, if no skirt, 1 inch below furniture bottom; leave 2 inches above deck. Pin-baste front to deck along curve; trim seam allowance to ½ inch.

Set-back arms cause the most common shape variation, the T-shaped deck. The deck piece won't lie flat for anchoring or pin-basting until you slit it where each arm curves out near the front. Before slitting, fold deck fabric back from and parallel to each arm so fabric lies flat on itself. Slit from fabric's edge to the curved crevice that separates arm from deck. Fold fabric out to cover deck's "ears"; if there is no separate front boxing piece, pin large horizontal dart where deck and wraparound front meet at side edge of T. Trim deck flaps to within 3 inches of crevice; trim dart to ½ inch. See "Slitting," page 66, for explanation of how to slit fabric sections when pin-basting inside arm to T-deck.

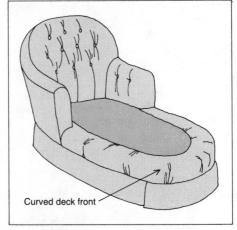

Curved deck on *chaise longue* requires separate front boxing piece.

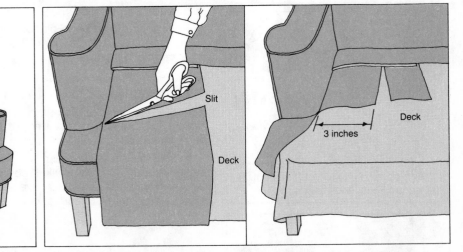

With set back arms, T-shaped deck section must be slit where arms begin to curve out. With deck fabric folded back on itself, slit to crevice curve; then fold fabric out to cover deck's "ears."

Inside back variations

How you pin-fit the inside back depends on its shape, its width, and whether the back cushion is attached or free.

Barrelback chair. During the blocking-out process you divided (with chalk) inside and outside back and arms into three or more vertical sections. Use your chalk marks now as pin-basting guides.

Pin arm and back sections in same sequence you'll be following for fully upholstered armchair. Most barrelbacks have no top boxing; you pin-baste inside back directly to outside back. Remember to start pin-basting at center back and work around to front—discard any excess fabric at curve ends.

Trim inside arm/back seam allowances to ½ inch down to point where bottom pin emerges. At that point, turn shears at a 45-degree angle and cut to end of section. This extra fabric makes inside arm/back tuck-in flaps flare out to fit rounded deck tuck-in. Pin-baste flaring flaps together ½ inch from edge; pin-baste complete inside arm/back tuck-in flap to deck. If inside arm/back tuck-in doesn't fit deck tuck-in, repin flaring flaps to fit; trim seam allowances to ½ inch.

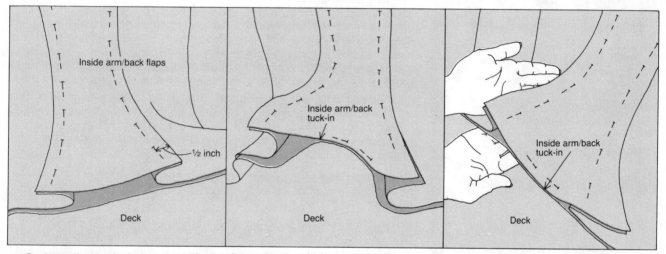

On barrelback chair, pin-baste flaring flaps together ½ inch from edges; pin-baste complete inside arm/back tuck-in flap to deck. You may need to repin and retrim flaring flaps to make inside arm/back tuck-in fit deck tuck-in.

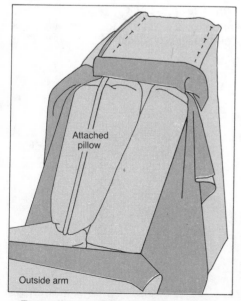

Ease slipcovering of attached pillow-back by ignoring pillow crevice.

Love seats, sofas, sofabeds. If you railroaded your fabric, you may wish to duplicate vertical upholstery welt on inside back or indicate grooves between attached pillows with vertical welt. When you anchor inside back, be sure to allow for a 1-inch-high vertical tuck wherever welt will occur. Snugly pin-baste these tucks, then trim each to a ½-inch seam allowance.

If fabric was vertically run over inside and outside back, chances are you blocked out more than one fabric width to span furniture's wide back, or to acknowledge vertical welt or grooves between attached pillows. As you anchor these sections, take care to position each so that matching motifs are at same height and at same distance from right and left edges.

No matter which way your fabric runs, remember to allow for height of missing deck cushions if you must center dominant motifs.

Tight back vs. attached pillowback. On a tight back, it's obvious that what you lean against will not pull free. Armless pieces of furniture, for instance, have tight backs. On many tight backs you can eliminate top boxing.

Attached pillowback furniture has back cushions that look as though they will pull free, but won't. Crevices on three sides separate each cushion from the back support. When you slipcover such furniture, the simplest method is to stretch fabric across top boxing and shoulders, ignoring pillow crevices. Follow upholstered seam on attached pillow when pin-fitting inside back to top boxing and shoulders; if your pillow has two seams, follow the one toward the front.

The deeper interior grooves that run vertically between attached pillows on love seats, sofas, and sofabeds are best ignored or indicated by welt—keeping a finished slipcover tucked into these grooves is very difficult.

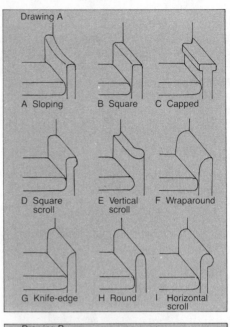

Drawing A

A Sloping   B Square   C Capped

D Square scroll   E Vertical scroll   F Wraparound

G Knife-edge   H Round   I Horizontal scroll

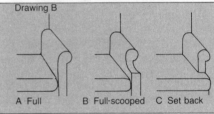

Drawing B

A Full   B Full-scooped   C Set back

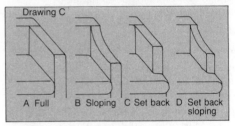

Drawing C

A Full   B Sloping   C Set back   D Set back sloping

Arm tops, sides, and fronts can vary greatly, requiring variations in pin-fitting techniques.

Arm variations

Of all furniture components, arms display the most variety. Drawing A shows the major configurations for arm tops, sides, and fronts. Any of Drawing A's shapes can be full, full-scooped, or set back (see Drawing B) and can begin at back height (Drawing C).

Don't let the wide range of arm shapes scare you. The following tips should help you to slipcover even the most unusual arm.

Arm tops. Several arm-top variations call for either top boxing or the standard inside/outside arm seam. If the arm you're slipcovering is sloping [a], you'll need to cut a top boxing strip 4 inches longer and 4 inches wider than upholstered strip. However, if arm is square [b], capped [c], square scroll [d], or vertical scroll [e], you have a choice: you can cut a top boxing strip, or you can save yourself work by ignoring boxing and pulling inside arm over the top and attaching it to outside arm as you would on a fully upholstered armchair. In either case, with capped or scroll arm tops, you make a slipcover that does not entirely hug the upholstery—pin-basting pulls the fabric taut, causing a hollow to form beneath scroll or cap.

Whether or not you ignore top boxing, if the arm is wraparound [f] or vertical scroll [e], make sure you pull enough inside arm fabric forward so you can wrap it around arm front. Before you pin-baste wraparound or vertical-scroll inside arm to outside arm, you'll need to make an unstitched dart at arm's top, unless you are using top boxing.

Arm/inside back. If you have to cut separate boxing for arm top, you won't need to slit upper inside arm—unless arm is a vertical scroll [e] on wing furniture.

If you're slipcovering wing furniture, substitute wing furniture Steps 1–6A or 1–6B, pages 78–79, for Step 24. Skip Step 25, then proceed to Step 26.

If your arm starts at back height, follow wing-furniture Step 6A or 6B only (substituting the word "arm" for "wing"); then proceed to Step 26.

Arm/T-deck. If slipcover for T-deck piece of furniture will *not* have front arm sections, wrap around and pin-baste inside arm to outside arm vertically to deck level. Fold inside arm tuck-in flap against arm at deck level. (For spring-edge deck *only,* push tuck-in ½ inch into crevice.) Pull up deck tuck-in so that bottom of its slit is 1 inch above deck. Hold slit edge against inside arm's tuck-in flap at point where inside arm meets front arm section.

Cut slit down inside arm flap, duplicating deck slit. Be sure inside arm slit reaches no farther down than 1 inch above deck—this extra fabric creates "give" across deck once inside arm is sewn to deck.

Now, matching slits, pin deck and inside arm flaps together with single pin. Trim flaps to within 3 inches of crevice; then follow directions under "Arm front/T-deck," page 77.

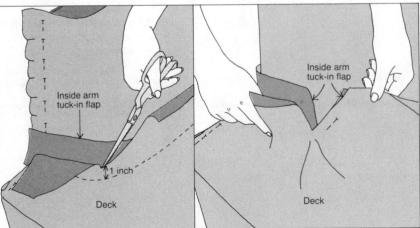

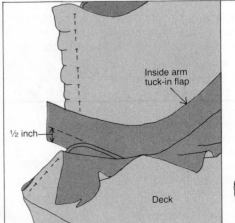

On spring-edge T-deck only, push tuck-in flap ½ inch into crevice.

Slit inside arm tuck-in flap to 1 inch above deck.

Pin deck and inside arm flaps together with single pin.

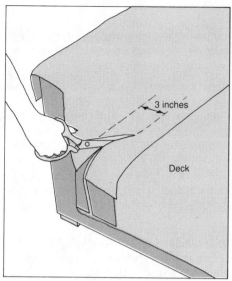

On arm/full arm deck, trim ½-inch allowance out to 3 inches toward back.

Arm/full-arm deck. If full-arm deck does *not* spring independently of the arm at arm's front (on most sofabeds it doesn't) and if it is bordered by full or full-scooped rather than setback arms (Drawing B, page 76), pin deck and inside arm tuck-in flaps together at arm's front with single pin. Starting at front, trim seam allowance to ½ inch at pin, tapering to 3-inch inside arm/deck tuck-in toward back. Then follow directions under "Arm front/full-arm deck," below.

Arm front/T-deck. Whether the T-deck does or does not spring independently determines how you pin-fit arm front area to deck. A no-spring-edge T-deck simply requires that you snugly pin-baste (with a single horizontal pin) arm front to T-deck flap where front meets deck. If you must cut separate front arm section ([a] through [d] and [g] through [i], Drawing A, page 76), remove cushion and cut front arm piece at least 4 inches longer than upholstered front arm. Baste this piece to inside/outside arm before pinning to deck.

Arm-front cutting and pinning techniques change somewhat when T-deck has spring edge. If you must cut *separate* front arm section ([a] through [d] and [g] through [i], Drawing A, page 76), make sure it is at least 5 inches longer than upholstered front arm section. Anchor so that bottom of separate or wraparound arm front extends at least 3 inches past deck crevice. Pin-baste separate front arm section to inside and outside arm. Where front arm section and inside arm join, push tuck-in 1 inch into crevice separating arm from deck, leaving out ½ inch for seam allowance. Now raise deck tuck-in slit 1 inch above deck. Pin slit's back edge to inside arm tuck-in flap where inside arm joins front arm section.

Push separate or wraparound arm front flap into crevice between arm front and deck so ½ inch is left out for seam allowance; pin-baste front flap to deck flap where front meets deck. Trim deck seam allowance to ½ inch. Keeping fold of arm front flap separated in crevice, attach (with single pin) front arm flap below deck level to lower outside arm. With single pin, attach other side of front arm flap to side of deck front below deck level. Continue pin-basting side of deck front to lower outside arm down to bottom of fabric. Trim down outside arm at front, from top of arm to bottom of fabric.

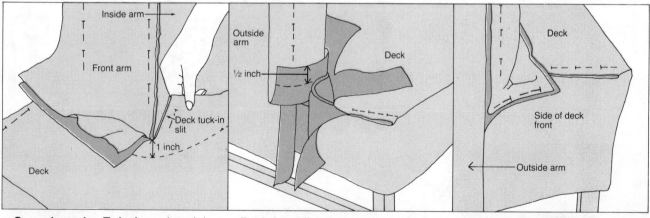

On spring-edge T-deck, push tuck-in 1 inch into crevice, raise deck slit 1 inch, and pin.

Push front flap into crevice so ½ inch is left out for seam allowance.

Pin front arm flap to lower outside arm and side of deck front.

Arm front/full-arm deck. If deck has no spring edge and is bordered by full or full-scooped arms, snugly pin-baste front arm section to inside arm down to level of deck. Continue basting front arm section to furniture front section until you reach bottom of fabric. Trim seam allowance to ½ inch (¾ inch on sofabeds, for zipper).

If deck is spring edge and is bordered by full or full-scooped arms that resemble [a] through [d] or [g] through [i] in Drawing A, page 76, follow Steps 28–31, pages 71–73, for fully upholstered armchair.

Other variations

Ottomans, sofabeds, and wings present some unique but not complex pin-fitting variations; right-side-out pin-fitting, used on asymmetrical furniture, involves only minor changes in basic pin-fitting techniques.

Ottomans. Of all furniture, ottomans are the simplest to pin-fit and sew. That's because, in most cases, you need neither darts nor zipper.

First anchor and pin-baste four sides (on round ottoman, four equal segments chalked vertically during blocking out). Then anchor top (on oblong ottoman, make sure motifs run in same direction as those on chair deck). Pin-baste top to sides.

Trim seam allowances to ½ inch. Only if upholstered top is slightly larger than ottoman's sides will you need a zipper; be sure to taper zipper allowance to ¾ inch (see zipper instructions for fully upholstered armchair, pages 73 and 94).

Sofabeds. Most wide furniture pieces need only one zipper, placed at either outside back edge. By giving a sofabed two extra zippers in front, each extending up front and along inside arm/deck crevice to back, you'll be able to pull out the bed without removing the slipcover.

If full or full-scooped arms border sofabed deck, follow instructions under "Arm/full-arm deck" and "Arm front/full-arm deck," page 77, with this exception: To accommodate zipper, trim sofabed seam allowance down front edge to ¾ inch, not ½ inch. Tuck-in extending to inside back along inside arm/deck crevice will hold rest of zipper; you prepare sofabed tuck-ins exactly as you prepare other tuck-ins.

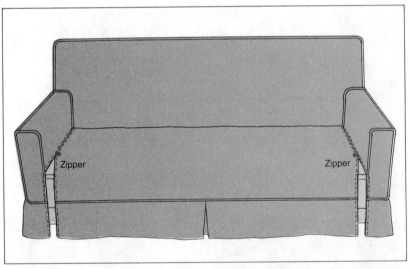

Zippers in front allow you to pull out sofabed without removing cover.

If set-back arms flank deck, creating a T-shape, you'll need to cut pieces from scrap fabric to cover each "ear" of the T and to help hold zipper. Each piece should be large enough to cover deck, front, and wraparound front piece on each ear, plus 2 inches at all edges. Anchor; then pin-baste each piece to main deck and front sections and make horizontal dart where deck and wraparound front meet at side edge of T. Trim zipper seam allowance to ¾ inch. Proceed to Step 28, page 71.

Wings. Think of wings as budding back-height arms that changed their minds. After pinning inside arm to outside arm, slit upper inside arm if needed; then shape and pin-fit inside wing as follows:

• *Step 1:* Block out inside wing at least 5 inches wider than upholstered wing's greatest width and 4 inches longer than upholstered wing's height.

• *Step 2:* Anchor inside wing with four pins. Be sure to leave 3-inch tuck-in flap if crevice exists between wing and inside back.

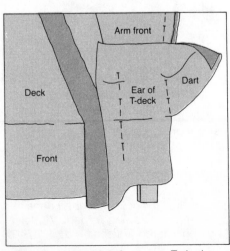

Scrap piece of fabric covers T-deck "ear" on sofabed.

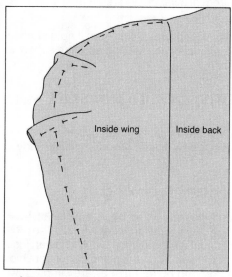

4 Form darts on inside wing to match those on upholstery.

- *Step 3:* Snugly pin-baste inside wing to outside wing. Pin from midpoint of wing's outside edge to bottom, then up and across wing top to back.

- *Step 4:* Reproduce probable two upholstered darts near top of inside wing.

- *Step 5:* Snugly pin-baste top (or top boxing) of inside arm to bottom of inside wing. You may need to slit fabric to help it hug wing's bottom curve.

- *Step 6A:* If crevice exists between wing and inside back, push inside wing and inside back fabric against, but not into, crevice. Pinch flaps together ⅘ of the way up from deck. Slit into flaps in a slight upward direction to within 1 inch of crevice. Make additional slits above as needed to help fabric hug crevice.

With single horizontal pin, baste tops of tuck-in below first cut. Snugly pin-baste seam allowance above cut(s) up to wing top.

Trim seam allowance above cut(s) to ½ inch. Trim tuck-in below to 3 inches (further pin-basting of tuck-in unnecessary). Trim inside arm/outside arm seam allowance, or inside arm/top boxing and outside arm/top boxing seam allowances to ½ inch.

- *Step 6B:* If *no* crevice exists between wing and inside back, slit fabric as needed to within 1 inch of groove that separates wing from inside back. Snugly pin-baste wing and inside arm to inside back.

Trim seam allowance to ½ inch. Trim inside arm/outside arm seam allowance, or inside arm/top boxing and outside arm/top boxing seam allowances to ½ inch.

Right-side-out pin-fitting

You can't pin-fit asymmetrical furniture wrong side out—if you did, the cover wouldn't fit when you reversed it. Instead, you must pin-fit with fabric's right side showing, following these steps:

- *Step 1:* Proceed exactly as described for wrong-side-out pin-fitting, except with right side of fabric out.

- *Step 2:* While slipcover is still on, cut two ¼-inch-deep notches with tips of shears in each pinned seam allowance. You will match these notches to realign seams when you repin.

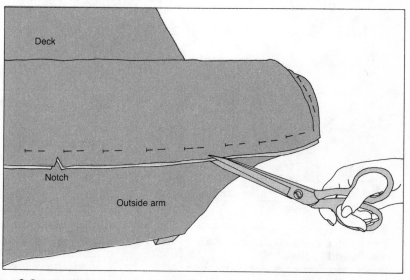

2 Cut two ¼-inch-deep notches in each pinned seam allowance.

- *Step 3:* Remove anchor pins and peel cover off furniture.

- *Step 4:* One seam allowance at a time, take out central pins, leaving one pin in at each end. On curves, take out only two pins at a time.

- *Step 5:* Push freed seam allowance to cover's wrong side. Match notches and repin allowance.
- *Step 6:* Pull the two end pins from allowance and repin on wrong side.
- *Step 7:* Repin remaining seams, one at a time.
- *Step 8:* After you've repinned cover on wrong side, turn it right side out and place on furniture. If its fit is too loose, see "Making sure the slipcover fits," page 73.

Cutting out cushions, boxing & skirt

Before sewing your slipcover, take a few minutes to cut out the cushions, boxing, and skirt. By doing these steps now, you'll have everything ready to sew when you need it.

How to cut out cushion covers & boxing

On most upholstered furniture, you'll find one of two basic cushion styles—the boxed cushion or the knife-edge cushion (with its variations). The most common style for a sofa or chair is the boxed cushion, which has an inset strip, usually 2 to 4 inches deep, that is sewn to the top and bottom cushion pieces. On a knife-edge cushion, top and bottom pieces are simply sewn together, creating a cushion that's deeper at the center and tapers toward the edges. Popular variations on the knife-edge cushion—the mock-box and soft-box cushions—have the depth of a boxed cushion without the inset; the fabric for the boxed area is part of the top and bottom pieces.

A zipper closure on the cushion will make it easy to remove the cover for cleaning. Before you cut boxing pieces, buy a heavy-duty zipper (available at upholstery supply stores and some fabric stores) for each cushion. A boxed cushion requires a zipper equal to the length of the cushion's back edge plus 6 inches so the zipper will extend around each back corner. For a knife-edge, mock-box, or soft-box cushion, use a zipper about 3 inches shorter than the *finished length* of the back edge (with a zipper any shorter, it would be difficult to insert the form or cushion).

Whatever the style of the cushion, run the fabric in the same direction as the slipcover (railroaded or vertically) and, on both top and bottom pieces, align large motifs or stripes with the inside back so that everything will match when the cushion is turned over.

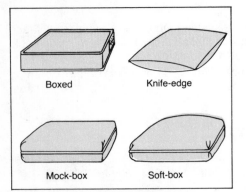

Boxed and knife-edge are the basic cushion styles; mock-box and soft-box are knife-edge variations.

Step-by-step: Cutting out a boxed cushion

1 Block out cushion top. On cushion, place a piece of fabric that's several inches larger all around. Anchor-pin.

2 Chalk corners and lines. Chalk corners and back edge, which may be curved slightly to fit chair's inside back. Remove fabric piece and chalk the other three edges, using a yardstick. Don't use cushion as guide for chalking these edges because cushion's straight lines may have become distorted over time.

3 Cut out cushion pieces. Adding a ½-inch seam allowance all around, cut out top cushion piece. Lay this piece on another piece of fabric and cut out an identical piece for bottom. *If your cushion is L-shaped, turn first (top) piece over on fabric (right sides facing) to cut bottom piece with the opposite orientation.* For a T-shaped cushion, fold each piece in half to check that corners are identical.

4 Measure and cut boxing pieces. For most chairs, you cut boxing strips across width of fabric (selvage to selvage). Cut 3 strips, each one as wide as the depth of finished boxing plus 1 inch for seam allowances. One piece will go across cushion's front and part way around both sides; the other two (each one folded in half length-

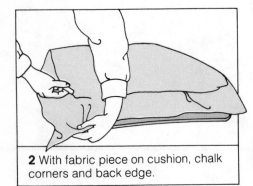

2 With fabric piece on cushion, chalk corners and back edge.

wise) together will make zipper boxing section for back. Use left-over pieces from back boxing sections (shorter than front), if needed, to piece onto front section.

For a T-shaped or L-shaped cushion, or a longer cushion such as a sofa cushion, you may need more than three boxing strips. Measure cushion's perimeter; divide that number by fabric width (excluding selvages) plus 1 inch for seam allowances. If the result is not a whole number, round it up to the next whole number. Add 1 to this number (the second zipper boxing strip) for the number of strips needed.

If you're railroading a fabric with one-way motifs, stripes, noticeable grainline, or nap, cut boxing strips on lengthwise grain of fabric (parallel to selvage). Cut two pieces zipper length plus 2 inches for back boxing section; cut one piece long enough to go across front and around sides to meet back boxing section, plus 2 inches.

Variations: Knife-edge, mock-box, and soft-box cushion. To make any of these three cushion styles, you should measure the cushion to be covered—it's easier and more accurate than blocking out on the cushion.

For a knife-edge cushion, measure the cushion length and width and chalk the dimensions directly onto your fabric, adding a ½-inch seam allowance on three edges and a ¾-inch seam allowance on the back edge where the zipper will go. Cut out top and bottom pieces.

Mock-box and soft-box top and bottom cushion pieces include the boxing area. Measure the cushion top. To each edge add half the depth of the boxing area, plus ½-inch seam allowances on three sides; on the back edge where the zipper will go, add a ¾-inch seam allowance. (For example, for a finished cushion 15 by 20 inches and 3 inches deep, each top and bottom piece should be 19¼ by 24 inches.) Cut out top and bottom pieces.

How to cut out a self-lined skirt

If you're going to make a skirt, we recommend that you make a self-lined one. Though it requires slightly more fabric than a hemmed skirt, a self-lined skirt hangs well, doesn't sport a hem, and is easy to make. On the other hand, if your fabric is unusually heavy or has a pattern that would show through on a self-lined skirt, it's better to line the skirt with cotton sateen drapery lining.

For a self-lined skirt, you'll want to cut strips of fabric that are as wide as twice the finished skirt height plus 1 inch (twice the ½-inch seam allowance). If your furniture will be on a deep pile carpet, you may want to subtract ¼ to ½ inch from the floor-to-finished-height measurement so the skirt won't drag on the carpet. The length of the strips (if railroading) or the number of strips (if running fabric vertically) depends on the style of skirt you're making.

Step-by-step: Cutting out a railroaded skirt

1 **Determine how many skirt strips you can cut from fabric width.** Divide width of fabric (without selvages) by width of skirt strips. For example, if fabric is 46 inches wide (without selvages) and you are making a 6-inch skirt, you will get three 13-inch strips (twice finished skirt height plus 1 inch) for the skirt, plus a 7-inch scrap strip. If fabric has dominant motifs or infrequent repeats, you may get only two skirt strips.

2 **Determine total length of strips you need.** First, measure perimeter of furniture at the level where you plan to attach skirt. Next, using one of the following formulas, calculate skirt fullness.

Straight tailored skirt = perimeter + 10 inches for each half of a pleat. Add 24 inches if you must match patterns.

Box-pleated or knife-pleated skirt = perimeter × 3¾.

Gathered skirt = perimeter × 3.

3 **Determine yardage.** To find out how much fabric you'll need to cut for skirt strips, divide the total length of strips you'll need by number of strips you can cut from the width of your fabric. If the result is not a whole number, round it up to the next whole number.

For example, let's say you are using fabric that's 46 inches wide (without selvages) to make a 6-inch knife-pleated skirt for a chair that has a perimeter of 112 inches. Multiply the perimeter by 3¾ (112 × 3¾ = 420 inches) and then divide by three strips (420 ÷ 3 = 140 inches). You will need 140 inches, or 3 yards and 32 inches (140 ÷ 36) of fabric for skirt strips. Dominant motifs and infrequent repeat patterns may require more yardage (see page 41).

4 **Prepare fabric.** Spread out required amount of fabric wrong side up and cut off one selvage.

5 **Measure and mark skirt strips.** Starting at the edge where you cut off selvage, measure and mark strips, using a yardstick or metal tape measure and chalk.

6 **Cut out strips.** Discard leftover scrap strip, if there is one.

7 **Press skirt strips.** Fold each strip in half lengthwise, right sides out, and press. Set aside until ready to make skirt.

Step-by-step: Cutting out a vertically run skirt

1 **Measure width of fabric without selvages.**

2 **Determine total length of strips needed.** First, measure perimeter of furniture at the level where you plan to attach skirt. Next, using one of the following formulas, calculate skirt fullness.

Straight tailored skirt = perimeter + 10 inches for each half of a pleat. Add 24 inches for hiding seams; add another 24 inches if you must match patterns.

Box-pleated or knife-pleated skirt = perimeter × 3¾.

Gathered skirt = perimeter × 3.

3 **Determine how many strips.** Divide the total length of strips you'll need by the width of fabric without selvages. If the result is not a whole number, round it up to the next whole number to learn how many skirt strips you'll need to cut.

4 **Determine yardage.** Multiply number of skirt strips you'll need by depth of each strip. Result tells you in inches how much fabric you'll need to cut for skirt. Dominant motifs and infrequent repeat patterns may require more yardage (see page 41).

5 **Prepare fabric.** Spread out required amount of fabric wrong side up and cut off both selvages.

6 **Measure, mark, and cut skirt strips.** Measure and mark strips, using a yardstick or metal tape measure and chalk. Cut out.

7 **Press skirt strips.** Fold each strip in half lengthwise, right sides out, and press. Set aside until ready to make skirt.

Welt

Traditionally, the seams of a slipcover are outlined with fabric-wrapped cord called welt, which reinforces the seams while adding a decorative touch.

The first sewing step in making a slipcover is to make the welt. You can skip this step, though, if you prefer to use ready-made welt that contrasts with or complements your slipcover fabric. For availability and color selection of ready-made welt, check upholstery supply stores and notions departments in fabric stores.

How much welt will you need?

To figure out how much welt you'll need, measure all the seams on your slipcover except those that will be tucked into crevices. Measure around the bottom (perimeter) of your slipcover, too, if you plan to have welt there. If you'll be making welted covers for knife-edge cushions, measure around the perimeter of each cushion; for boxed cushions, measure around the boxing and then double the figure. Adding all these measurements—plus an extra foot for good measure—will tell you how much cord or ready-made welt you'll need to buy.

Making your own welt

If you plan to make your own welt, buy plain cord—sometimes called cable cord—from a fabric store. You may find several sizes and types of cord; for most slipcover projects you should use ¼-inch-thick cotton or polyester cord.

Bias casing

To ensure that welt fits smoothly along the curves and corners of your slipcover, use a bias-cut casing of fabric to cover the cord. The bias casing should be wide enough to wrap around the cord with enough extra for twice the width of the seam allowance. The directions in this book, which are based on ¼-inch-thick cord and ½-inch seam allowances, use bias casing that's 1⅝ inches wide.

You can make the casing as one continuous bias strip or as separate bias strips that you join together.

Step-by-step: Making continuous bias casing

In terms of both fabric and effort, this method for making a continuous bias casing is very efficient. The chart on page 85 shows the approximate number of yards of continuous bias strip you will get from a given amount of fabric.

1 **Make bias cylinder.** Trim off selvages and fold fabric in half across shorter dimension, right sides together. Stitch a ½-inch seam around three sides of the rectangle.

Trim all four corners as shown, cutting through stitching.

Picking up two diagonally opposite corners, (C and D), fold fabric rectangle so it forms two triangles. Carefully insert shears into end of fold and cut all the way across, through *one* layer of fabric.

Pick up bottom corners (A and B) and slowly pull them, shaking out fabric; bottom corners are now top corners of a rectangle, with a fold along the top.

Cut top fold open so fabric is now a bias cylinder with a fold on each end. Press seam allowances open and trim upper and lower edges of cylinder to make them even.

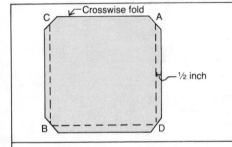

1 Right sides together, fold fabric in half; stitch three sides; trim corners.

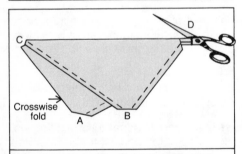

1 Pick up C and D, forming fold at top; cut across fold through *one* fabric layer.

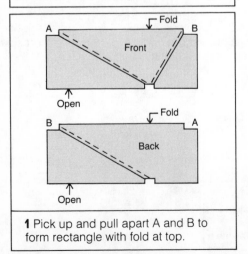

1 Pick up and pull apart A and B to form rectangle with fold at top.

2 **Measure and mark strips.** Using chalk or pencil, draw a line across the cylinder 6 inches from the left side fold. Measure and mark 1⅝-inch-wide strips from the 6-inch line to the opposite end. If you end with a fraction of a strip on the bottom, cut it all the way off cylinder and discard.

3 **Cut strips.** Cut along marks from right-hand fold to 6-inch line, cutting through both thicknesses of cylinder. After cutting all strips, refold cylinder so that uncut portion is centered on top.

   Using a straightedge, mark a diagonal line from end of topmost cut to a point on upper edge of cylinder even with opposite ends of cuts. Next, mark a diagonal line from end of second cut to opposite end of first cut. Continue marking until all cuts are connected with diagonal lines.

   Cutting through one layer of fabric, cut along each diagonal line. As you do this, casing will fall into one continuous bias strip.

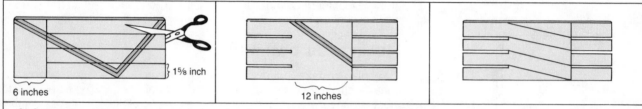

2–3 On bias cylinder, measure and mark strips 1⅝ inches wide, from 6-inch line to opposite end; cut along marks and refold so uncut portion is on top. Mark and cut diagonal lines between ends of cuts.

Step-by-step: Making separate bias strips

If you need only a small amount of welt, you may want to piece together several separate bias strips rather than make a bias cylinder. Here's how to cut and piece together separate strips from fabric scrap.

1 **Establish bias line.** Fold a corner of the fabric so that selvage aligns with crosswise cut; cut fabric along bias fold.

2 **Measure, mark, and cut strips.** Using diagonal cut as a guideline, measure and mark 1⅝-inch-wide strips parallel to the cut. Stop when bottom edge of strip is no longer on crosswise cut (strips are easiest to join when their ends are on crosswise grain of fabric). Cut along lines.

3 **Join strips.** With right sides together, position two strips at a right angle, offset slightly as shown, and join with a ¼-inch seam; press seam open. Sew all strips together in this manner.

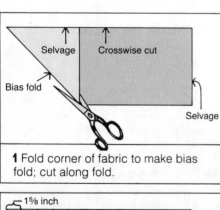

1 Fold corner of fabric to make bias fold; cut along fold.

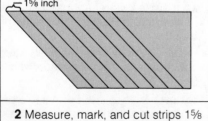

2 Measure, mark, and cut strips 1⅝ inches wide, parallel to bias cut.

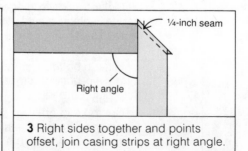

3 Right sides together and points offset, join casing strips at right angle.

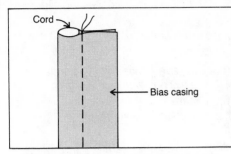

Bias casing is wrapped around and sewn close to cord.

Assembling welt

Lay the cord along the center of the wrong side of your bias casing. Fold the casing over the cord, aligning raw edges.

Set your sewing machine for the longest stitch and attach the zipper foot. Sew through the casing close to the cord—but not crowding it, since you'll later want to stitch the slipcover seams between the welt seam and the cord. One way to gauge yourself is to put a strip of masking tape with its right-hand edge just inside the ½-inch seam guide on your sewing machine. Sewing with this guide will ensure that the first stitching won't show after you sew the ½-inch slipcover seams.

With one hand in front and one hand in back of the needle, gently stretch the bias casing as you sew. This will help the welt lie smoothly in the slipcover seams.

YARDS OF FABRIC	APPROXIMATE NUMBER OF RUNNING YARDS OF 1⅝-INCH-WIDE CONTINUOUS BIAS CASING		
	36" fabric	48" fabric	54" fabric
¼ yard	4½ yards	5½ yards	7 yards
½ yard	10 yards	13 yards	14 yards
¾ yard	16 yards	20 yards	22 yards
1 yard	22 yards	26 yards	29½ yards

Putting it all together

A slipcover isn't difficult to sew, but it is bulky and can be cumbersome to work with. Try to arrange a sewing area with plenty of flat space around your machine for the slipcover to rest on as you sew.

Sewing in general

If you're making a slipcover with welt in the seams, use a zipper foot to sew the entire slipcover. On a no-welt slipcover, you can use a regular presser foot for all stitching except installing the zipper.

All sewing of a slipcover is done with a straight stitch; 10 is a good stitch length for lightweight fabric, 8 for medium, and 6 for heavy fabric. Check the tension of your stitching by sewing through several thicknesses of scrap slipcover fabric.

As you sew sections together, backstitch the end of any seam that isn't crossed by another seam.

Transition from pin-basting to sewing. With our method of making a slipcover, you go directly from a pin-basted cover to a sewn cover. You remove the basting pins as you sew, and you use the holes made by the basting pins as a sewing guide. If you are adding welt, slip it into the seams as you sew (see page 86). Where there is a little extra fullness in one of the slipcover pieces, take out the basting pins, distribute the fullness evenly, and repin, placing the pins close together, perpendicular to the seamline. Sew with the fuller section on the bottom and the flatter section on top.

Plan for sewing. Before taking your pin-fitted slipcover off the furniture, study it to familiarize yourself with all the seams and how they fit together. Often the pin-fitted cover itself suggests a logical order for sewing the seams.

Sew darts first. It's best to go through your pin-basted slipcover and sew all darts first so you won't unexpectedly come across a pinned dart while

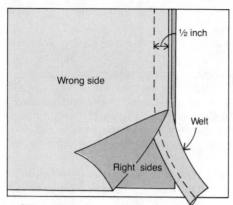

Slip welt between slipcover pieces as you sew seam.

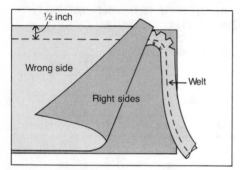

To turn a corner, make diagonal cuts into welt seam allowance.

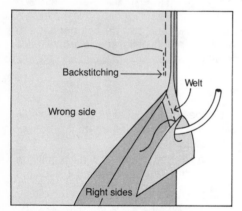

To join welt, remove stitching from end and pull cord aside.

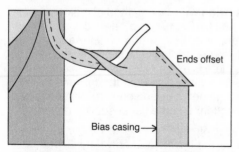

Place casing ends at 90-degree angle, with points offset.

you're sewing a seam. (For an exception to this rule, see "Sewing slipcover variations," page 97.)

Sew each dart from the fabric's edge to the dart's tip. Backstitch at the tip; trim seam allowance to ¼ inch.

Sewing seams. First sew seams that will have no welt (for example, deck to inside arm). Then sew seams following the numbered steps on page 87.

As in the rest of this book, a fully upholstered armchair is the example. For other furniture pieces, read the armchair instructions first; then see "Sewing slipcover variations," pages 97–98.

How to work with welt. Here are some special techniques you'll need if you're making a slipcover with welt:

• *Slipping welt into seams:* Put your welt in a neat pile on the floor near your feet. As you remove basting pins, slip welt into seam, aligning raw edges of welt with raw edges of slipcover seam allowances. Sew seam, stitching through slipcover sections and welt.

• *Clipping welt seam allowance:* Any time welt doesn't lie flat, make several diagonal cuts into seam allowance *almost* to the stitching. When turning a corner with welt, make three diagonal cuts—one right at the corner and one on each side of the corner cut.

• *When welt crosses welt:* To reduce the bulk of welt crossing welt, remove ½ inch of *cord* from bottom welt. Grasp end of cord, pull it out of its casing, cut off ½ inch, and smooth out casing.

Try to anticipate when one welted seam is going to be crossed by another. As you prepare to sew the seam that will be crossed, pull out and cut off ½ inch of cord at beginning of seam so the first ½ inch of casing contains no cord. At end of seam, cut off welt even with slipcover seam allowance, then pull out and cut off the last ½ inch of cord.

• *How to join welt:* Follow this procedure if the piece of welt you're using is not long enough to reach the end of the seam: about 4 inches before you come to end of welt, stop sewing, backstitch, break threads, and take slipcover out from under sewing machine needle. Remove last 3 inches of welt stitching and pull cord aside; then cut end of bias casing at a 45-degree angle. On a new piece of prepared welt, do the same on first 3 inches.

Place ends of two casings (offset slightly) so that strips form a 90-degree angle, with right sides together; join with a ¼-inch seam and finger-press seam open.

Cut joining ends of cord diagonally so they fit together well. Unravel a few threads from each cord end so that when casing is sewn over the cord, the threads will be caught in seam. Using a long stitch, sew casing seam. Put slipcover back under needle, reset stitch length, and continue sewing seam.

When welt encircles the edges of a cushion or the top of an ottoman, you need to use a special technique where welt ends meet. See "Join welt ends," page 99.

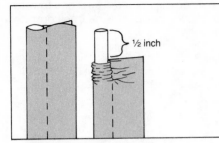

Before sewing a welted seam, pull out and cut off ½ inch of cord.

Step-by-step: Sewing a slipcover with skirt & welt for a fully upholstered armchair

Note: Each time you're about to sew a welted seam, first be sure to pull out and cut off ½ inch of cord from end of welt; then sew seam and cut off other end of welt even with seam allowance; finally, pull out and cut off last ½ inch of cord. (Exceptions occur for zipper and skirtline welt.)

1 **Spring-edge dart.** Sew dart at front corner of spring edge. Repeat on other corner.

2 **Inside arm to deck.** Sew tuck-in joining inside arm to deck, stitching from front to back. Repeat on other side.

3 **Shoulder to top boxing.** Sew shoulder to top boxing, with welt. Repeat on other shoulder.

4 **Up and around inside back.** Join shoulder/top boxing/shoulder piece to inside back by sewing up shoulder, across top, and down other shoulder, with welt. As you sew, turn seam allowances of already sewn shoulder/top boxing seams toward top boxing.

5 **Inside arm to inside back and shoulder.** Sew inside arm to inside back and shoulder, with welt. As you sew, turn seam allowances of already sewn inside back/shoulder seam toward shoulder. Repeat on other inside arm.

6 **Inside back to deck.** Sew tuck-in joining inside back to deck, without welt.

7 **Inside arm and shoulder to outside arm.** Sew inside arm to outside arm and shoulder to outside arm, with welt. Stitch from front to back. As you sew, turn seam allowances of already sewn inside arm/shoulder seam toward shoulder. Repeat on other arm.

8 **Front arm section.** Sew front arm section to inside and outside arm, with welt. As you sew, turn seam allowances of already sewn inside/outside arm seam toward outside arm. Repeat on other front arm section.

9 **Up and around outside back.** Start this seam at the bottom of the side that will have zipper (you can tell which side will have zipper because it has no pins). Lay welt over seamline you chalked during pin-fitting. Sew welt to right side of outside arm and shoulder for entire length of zipper opening. When you get to where the closed end of zipper will be, include the outside back in seam.

Now, with welt in seam, sew last 1 inch of shoulder to outside back, top boxing to outside back; sew other shoulder and outside arm to outside back. As you sew, turn seam allowances of already sewn outside arm/shoulder seam toward outside arm, and shoulder/top boxing seam toward top boxing.

10 **Welt around skirtline.** You sew welt to slipcover's right side around skirtline before attaching skirt. First remove cord from bottom ¾ inch of zipper welt so skirtline welt can easily cross it. Pull out and remove the first 1 inch of cord from starting end of skirtline welt. Align welt and slipcover seam allowances and stitch. As you sew across welt that runs down zipper seam allowance, turn rounded part of zipper welt so that it points toward the opening. When you reach other side of zipper opening, cut off welt even with seam allowance, remove the last 1 inch of cord, and finish stitching.

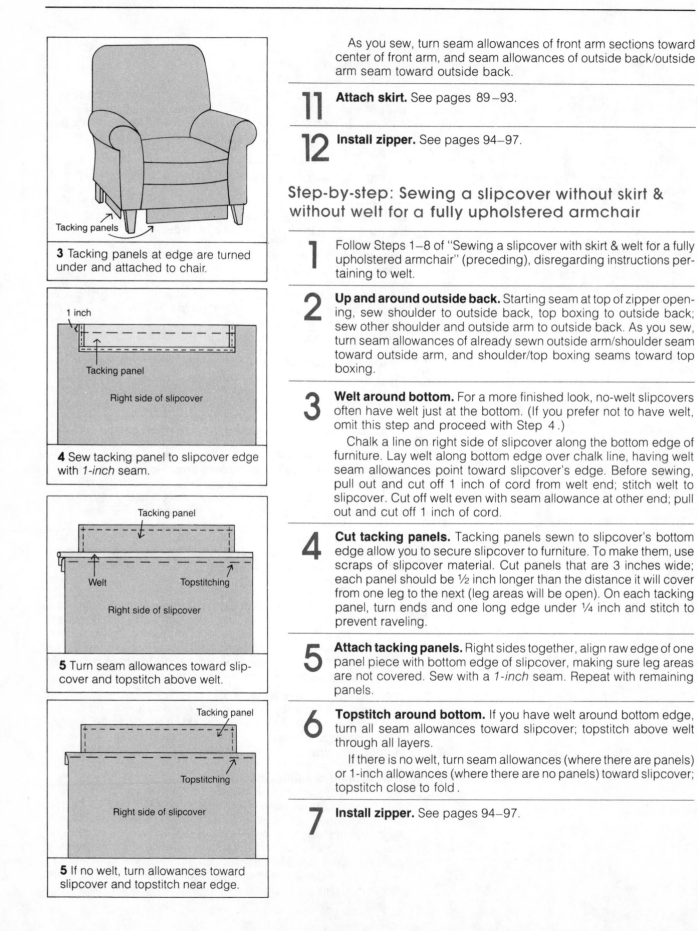

3 Tacking panels at edge are turned under and attached to chair.

1 inch

Tacking panel

Right side of slipcover

4 Sew tacking panel to slipcover edge with *1-inch* seam.

Tacking panel

Welt   Topstitching

Right side of slipcover

5 Turn seam allowances toward slipcover and topstitch above welt.

Tacking panel

Topstitching

Right side of slipcover

5 If no welt, turn allowances toward slipcover and topstitch near edge.

As you sew, turn seam allowances of front arm sections toward center of front arm, and seam allowances of outside back/outside arm seam toward outside back.

11 **Attach skirt.** See pages 89–93.

12 **Install zipper.** See pages 94–97.

Step-by-step: Sewing a slipcover without skirt & without welt for a fully upholstered armchair

1 Follow Steps 1–8 of "Sewing a slipcover with skirt & welt for a fully upholstered armchair" (preceding), disregarding instructions pertaining to welt.

2 **Up and around outside back.** Starting seam at top of zipper opening, sew shoulder to outside back, top boxing to outside back; sew other shoulder and outside arm to outside back. As you sew, turn seam allowances of already sewn outside arm/shoulder seam toward outside arm, and shoulder/top boxing seams toward top boxing.

3 **Welt around bottom.** For a more finished look, no-welt slipcovers often have welt just at the bottom. (If you prefer not to have welt, omit this step and proceed with Step 4.)

Chalk a line on right side of slipcover along the bottom edge of furniture. Lay welt along bottom edge over chalk line, having welt seam allowances point toward slipcover's edge. Before sewing, pull out and cut off 1 inch of cord from welt end; stitch welt to slipcover. Cut off welt even with seam allowance at other end; pull out and cut off 1 inch of cord.

4 **Cut tacking panels.** Tacking panels sewn to slipcover's bottom edge allow you to secure slipcover to furniture. To make them, use scraps of slipcover material. Cut panels that are 3 inches wide; each panel should be ½ inch longer than the distance it will cover from one leg to the next (leg areas will be open). On each tacking panel, turn ends and one long edge under ¼ inch and stitch to prevent raveling.

5 **Attach tacking panels.** Right sides together, align raw edge of one panel piece with bottom edge of slipcover, making sure leg areas are not covered. Sew with a *1-inch* seam. Repeat with remaining panels.

6 **Topstitch around bottom.** If you have welt around bottom edge, turn all seam allowances toward slipcover; topstitch above welt through all layers.

If there is no welt, turn seam allowances (where there are panels) or 1-inch allowances (where there are no panels) toward slipcover; topstitch close to fold.

7 **Install zipper.** See pages 94–97.

Skirts

The following directions assume that you are making a self-lined skirt and that you have prepared the skirt strips as described on pages 80–82. If you're making a skirt for an ottoman slipcover that doesn't require a zipper, see "Ottoman variation," page 93.

Step-by-step: Making a gathered skirt

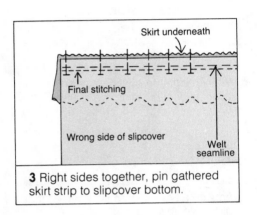

3 Right sides together, pin gathered skirt strip to slipcover bottom.

Soft fabrics in solid colors or small patterns work well for gathered skirts.

1 **Join skirt strips.** Make one long skirt strip by unfolding skirt strips and joining ends, right sides together, with ½-inch seams. Press seam allowances open, refold skirt in half lengthwise, and repress lengthwise fold.

2 **Gather skirt.** With sewing machine set for longest stitch, sew two rows of gathering stitches—one row on the ½-inch seamline at top of skirt, the second row ¼ inch above the first. It's best to interrupt stitching occasionally to make gathering easier.

Working from both ends, pull on bobbin threads to gather skirt to length that approximately equals distance around bottom of slipcover.

3 **Pin skirt to slipcover.** With right sides together, and inserting pins from wrong side of slipcover, pin skirt to bottom of slipcover, aligning raw edges. Distribute fullness until skirt fits slipcover.

4 **Sew skirt to slipcover.** With wrong side of slipcover on top and skirt underneath, sew skirt to slipcover, stitching between welt seamline and cord. If no welt, stitch with ½-inch seam.

Step-by-step: Making a knife-pleated skirt

3 Starting ¾ inch from end, measure and mark pleat width on skirt strip.

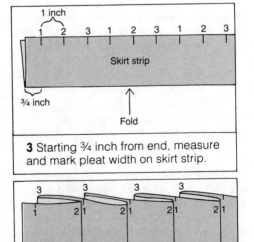

4 Form pleats by making folds at numbers 2 and 3.

You can hide skirt strip seams behind knife pleats by making slight adjustments in pleat size where needed.

1 **Join skirt strips.** Make one long skirt strip by unfolding skirt strips and joining ends, right sides together, with ½-inch seams. Press seam allowances open, refold skirt in half lengthwise, and repress lengthwise fold.

2 **Determine pleat size.** A knife-pleated skirt can have pleats varying from small, even tucks to full-size pleats 1½ to 3 inches wide. Base pleat size on what looks good in proportion to skirt height.

3 **Measure and mark pleats.** Once you decide on a finished size for pleats, measure and mark pleat width along skirt strip, starting ¾ inch (zipper seam allowance) from either end. Number the marks from 1 to 3, repeating until you just pass the first seam.

4 **Form pleats.** Going back to end where you started, make folds at numbers 2 and 3 as shown in drawing. As you form each pleat, pin it in place. If first seam falls between numbers 1 and 2, hide it by making preceding inside fold (between numbers 3 and 1) larger or smaller.

Mark and number divisions from edge of last pleat just past next seam, then repeat the division-marking and seam-hiding process for entire length of skirt as you form pleats.

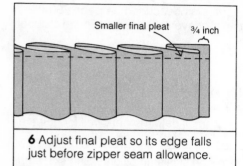

6 Adjust final pleat so its edge falls just before zipper seam allowance.

5 **Baste pleats in place.** Make a single row of stitching on the ½-inch seamline of skirt, to baste pleats in place. Remove pins.

6 **Adjust skirt length.** Measure around bottom edge of slipcover where skirt will go. Measure an equal distance on pleated skirt. Take out stitching at top of last pleat and adjust pleat size so edge of pleat falls just before ¾-inch zipper seam allowance. Cut off skirt, allowing for ¾-inch seam allowance. Rebaste top of adjusted pleat.

7 **Press pleats.** Press pleats (unless they are small tuck-pleats).

8 **Pin skirt to slipcover.** With right sides together, and inserting pins from wrong side of slipcover, pin skirt to bottom of slipcover, aligning raw edges.

9 **Sew skirt to slipcover.** With wrong side of slipcover on top and skirt underneath, sew skirt to slipcover, stitching between welt seamline and cord. If no welt, stitch with ½-inch seam.

Step-by-step: Making a box-pleated skirt

Measuring and forming pleats on a box-pleated skirt can be tricky because pleat edges should meet at corners.

1 **Join skirt strips.** Make one long skirt strip by unfolding skirt strips and joining ends, right sides together, with ½-inch seams. Press seam allowances open, refold skirt in half lengthwise, and repress lengthwise fold.

2 **Determine number and size of pleats.** Base pleat size on fabric motifs and what looks good in proportion to skirt height. Start with a 3-inch pleat and then go larger or smaller until you find a size you like. (Finished pleat size may actually be a little larger or smaller than originally planned because you will be adjusting to make edges of two pleats meet on a corner.)

Next find number of pleats for each side of furniture piece—front and back may not be the same; sides are likely to be identical. The first step is to divide length of one side by your chosen pleat size. For example, if one side is 25½ inches long and you want 3-inch pleats, you will have 8.5 ($25.5 \div 3 = 8.5$) pleats on that side. Since you can't have a fraction of a pleat, you must decide to have either 8 pleats, each 3.2 inches wide ($25.5 \div 8 = 3.2$), or 9 pleats, each 2.8 inches wide ($25.5 \div 9 = 2.8$).

Unless all four sides of your furniture piece are the same length (measure each to be certain), you'll have to make similar computations for the other sides. It is likely that finished pleat size for remaining two sides will be slightly larger or smaller than that for first two. For example, if each of the other two sides is 17½ inches wide, you'll be making 6 pleats ($17.5 \div 3 = 5.8$, rounded off to 6), each 2.9 inches wide ($17.5 \div 6 = 2.9$). Don't be concerned; when skirt is finished and sewn to slipcover, the difference between pleats that are 2.8 inches and ones that are 2.9 inches wide will not be visible. Because ordinary rulers don't show tenths of inches, we've provided a drawing that does; use it as a pattern to help you measure.

```
  1 2 3 4 5 6 7 8 9
                1          2          3          4
```

Tenths of an inch marked on this "ruler" will help you mark pleat divisions.

3 **Make a cardboard template.** The easiest way to mark divisions for pleats is to make a cardboard template three times the size of a finished pleat (each box pleat requires three times its width in fabric). On lightweight cardboard, mark and number 6 divisions, *each* half the size of a pleat. If you'll have pleats of two different sizes, make another template with pleat size divisions.

4 **Measure and mark pleats for one side of furniture.** Starting ¾ inch (zipper seam allowance) from either end, mark sets of divisions on your long skirt strip until you reach first seam.

5 **Form pleats for one side of furniture.** Going back to end where you started, make folds at numbers 2, 3, 5, and 6 as shown in drawing; pin pleats in place as you go. If first seam falls *between* numbers 3 and 5, or *on* number 1, 3, or 5, take out seam and rejoin skirt strips so seam will be hidden (between numbers 1 and 3, or 5 and 1). Finish marking divisions and forming pleats, hiding seams where needed, until you have correct number for that side.

After making pleats for one side, measure pleated section of skirt against slipcover section to make sure edges of pleats line up with slipcover corner seams on each end.

6 **Measure, mark, and form pleats for remaining sides.** Repeat Steps 4 and 5 for each remaining side, marking divisions from edge of last pleat. After you've pleated and measured last side of skirt, mark a ¾-inch zipper seam allowance and cut off remaining skirt strip.

7 **Baste pleats in place.** With a single row of stitching on the ½-inch seamline of skirt, baste pleats in place. Remove pins.

8 **Press pleats.** Press pleats in skirt, or leave unpressed if you prefer a softer look.

9 **Pin skirt to slipcover.** With right sides together, and inserting pins from wrong side of slipcover, pin skirt to bottom of slipcover, aligning raw edges.

10 **Sew skirt to slipcover.** With wrong side of slipcover on top and skirt underneath, sew skirt to slipcover, using as a sewing guide the row of stitching that joins welt to slipcover.

Step-by-step: Making a straight tailored skirt

Tailored skirts usually have inverted pleats at their corners and sometimes in between. (An inverted corner pleat looks the same as the reverse side of a box pleat.)

1 **Plan on paper first.** The best way to plan where to join skirt strips for a tailored skirt is to make a sketch of furniture's perimeter that shows where each pleat will occur and the distance in inches between pleats.

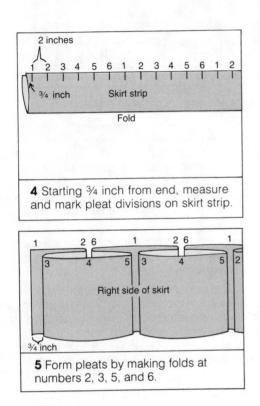

4 Starting ¾ inch from end, measure and mark pleat divisions on skirt strip.

5 Form pleats by making folds at numbers 2, 3, 5, and 6.

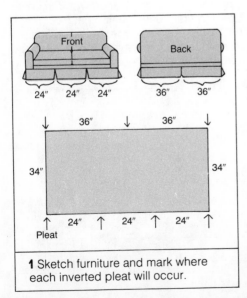

1 Sketch furniture and mark where each inverted pleat will occur.

Next, make a sketch of the continuous skirt strip. Mark pleats, as well as spaces between pleats, allowing 10 inches for each half pleat and 20 inches for each full pleat.

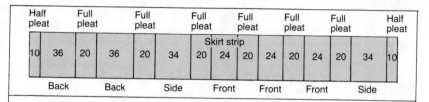

Half pleat	Full pleat		Full pleat		Full pleat		Full pleat		Full pleat		Full pleat		Full pleat		Half pleat
10	36	20	36	20	34	20	24	20	24	20	24	20	34	10
	Back		Back		Side		Front		Front		Front		Side	

1 Sketch skirt strip, marking pleats and spaces between pleats.

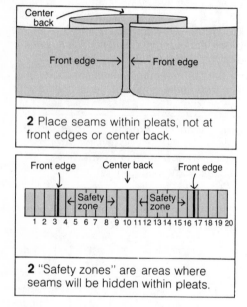

2 Place seams within pleats, not at front edges or center back.

2 "Safety zones" are areas where seams will be hidden within pleats.

2 Make a joining plan. You must plan carefully where to join skirt sections so seams are hidden within pleats (preferably not at either of the two front edges of a pleat or at its center back). Therefore, if you are allowing 20 inches for a pleat, you have a "safety zone" for seams between inches 4–9 and 11–16 (see drawing for clarification).

You may have to piece skirt strips to get the length you need for each section between corners. If you do, be sure to add this piece so its seams fall within "safety zone."

To match pattern, hold up a skirt strip to each slipcover section (front, sides, back) and move it horizontally until you get pattern match you want. Label each strip so you'll know which section it matches, then place a pin at point where strip matches center of slipcover section. All measurements for section length and for placement of seams and inserts should be taken from this center pin.

Before joining skirt strips, make a drawing that shows locations of seams and/or inserts. There is no extra fabric for seam allowances—these are taken out of the 10 inches allowed for each half pleat.

3 Join skirt strips. Following joining plan, make one long skirt strip by unfolding skirt strips and joining ends, right sides together, with ½-inch seams. Press seam allowances open, refold skirt in half lengthwise, and repress lengthwise fold.

4 Pin skirt to slipcover. With right sides together, and inserting pins from wrong side of skirt, pin skirt to bottom of slipcover, matching patterns, if necessary. Leaving first 10-inch half pleat free, place your first pin ¾ inch in from zipper opening edge. At each pleat, pin up to the two folds that come together, but leave rest of pleat loose. Place last pin ¾ inch in from other zipper opening edge, leaving last half pleat free.

5 **Sew skirt to slipcover.** With wrong side of skirt on top and slipcover underneath, sew skirt to slipcover, using as a sewing guide the stitching that joins welt to slipcover. Sew each flat section up to the pin at each pleat fold, then backstitch, break off stitching and resume sewing at other pleat fold.

6 **Form pleats.** To form half-pleats at zipper opening edges, fold skirt back over itself and then toward zipper opening, aligning raw edges of skirt end and zipper seam allowance. To form full pleats, finger-press pleat folds where pins are. Next, center loose part of pleat so there is an equal amount of fabric on each side of point where pleat folds meet. Pin pleats in place.

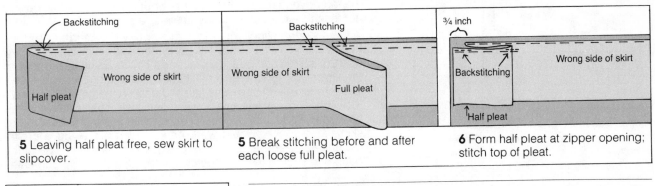

5 Leaving half pleat free, sew skirt to slipcover.

5 Break stitching before and after each loose full pleat.

6 Form half pleat at zipper opening; stitch top of pleat.

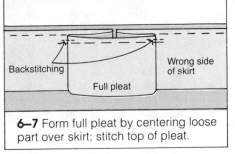

6–7 Form full pleat by centering loose part over skirt; stitch top of pleat.

7 **Finish sewing pleats.** Sew tops of pleats along ½-inch seamline, backstitching each end.

8 **Press pleats.** With skirt stitched to slipcover, press pleats.

9 **Ottoman variation.** For an ottoman slipcover without a zipper, you'll have to sew skirt ends together before you make pleats or gathers. Disregard references to ¾-inch zipper seam allowance as you follow instructions. If pleating skirt, start measuring and marking your pleats from any point at least 3 inches away from a seam. When you have pleated entire skirt strip loop, measure it against circumference of your slipcover. Adjust size of last few pleats to make skirt fit slipcover and to hide last seam.

PUTTING ON THE SLIPCOVER

You've finished sewing and you're just about ready for the moment you've been waiting for—seeing the slipcover on your furniture. The only thing left to do is to touch it up where necessary with an iron, and be sure that all pleats are sharply pressed.

To put on the slipcover, stand at the back of your furniture and, with the zipper open, drop the cover over the back of the furniture. Work the slipcover in place along the top, the shoulders, and down the back.

Next, put the cover over each arm. Working in front of the furniture, adjust the cover across the front and smooth the deck toward the back. Use your fingers or a 12-inch ruler to push tuck-in allowances into crevices.

Holding the bottom edges closed with one hand, pull down the zipper tab with the other. On a skirtless cover, tuck the excess zipper length up and under itself.

For a skirted or skirtless slipcover, follow the instructions on page 95 for securing the slipcover to the furniture.

Once your slipcover is in place, stand back and admire your work. Check to see if the welt is straight and if the slipcover looks snug. You can improve the fit by placing rolls of paper or foam in the tuck-ins.

If the fabric has wrinkles, you can wait several days—they may disappear. Otherwise, iron the slipcover right on the furniture.

Most slipcover fabrics are treated with a soil-resistant finish. If yours isn't, use a soil-resistant spray once the slipcover is on the furniture.

To ensure maximum wear, have your slipcover dry-cleaned—and don't wait until it's badly soiled. Slipcovers made of bedsheets and machine washable fabrics may be washed, but the fabric will lose some of its crispness.

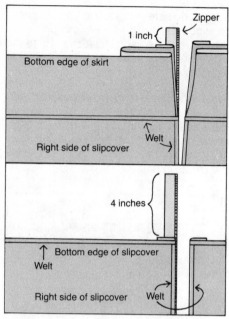

One inch of zipper extends past skirt bottom; a skirtless slipcover needs 4 inches of zipper beyond bottom.

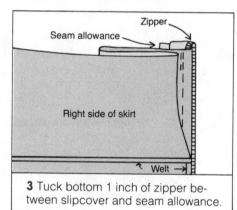

3 Tuck bottom 1 inch of zipper between slipcover and seam allowance.

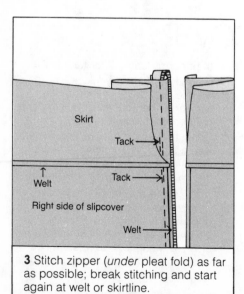

3 Stitch zipper (*under* pleat fold) as far as possible; break stitching and start again at welt or skirtline.

Zippers

Here are step-by-step instructions for installing a zipper in a welted slipcover and in a no-welt slipcover, followed by instructions for installing the two front zippers in a sofabed.

Step-by-step: Installing a zipper in a welted slipcover

On a skirted or skirtless slipcover, you'll have ½ inch of zipper at the top beyond the point where the zipper opening ends. You sew across this extra zipper length to secure zipper ends.

On a skirted slipcover, 1 inch of zipper will extend beyond the bottom of the skirt; this end will get turned and sewn when you sew up the first side and down the second side. On a skirtless slipcover, the zipper will extend about 4 inches past the bottom of the slipcover; once the slipcover is finished and on the furniture, you will tuck the extra zipper length up under itself. That extra length is necessary, because a zipper that reached just to the bottom of a skirtless slipcover would work open. If you are using a cut-to-measure zipper, handstitch across the teeth on each side of the bottom to secure the slide before tucking the zipper underneath.

1 **Press under seam allowances.** If slipcover has a skirt, first extend zipper seam allowance chalk lines from slipcover onto skirt. Then, on a skirted or skirtless slipcover, turn under and press seam allowances along chalk lines on both edges.

2 **Position zipper.** Working from right side of slipcover, place closed zipper face up under one side of zipper opening so that pressed edge (or welt, if it occurs on that side) almost covers zipper teeth. Place end of zipper tape 1 inch beyond bottom of skirt or 4 inches beyond bottom of skirtless slipcover.

3 **Stitch up zipper.** *On a skirted slipcover*, turn up bottom 1 inch of zipper tape, tucking it between slipcover and seam allowance. Using zipper foot, start sewing ¾ inch from bottom, backstitch, and continue sewing up zipper ¼ inch in from pressed edge (or, if welt occurs on that side, along welt, using welt seam as a guide). Keep pressed edge almost covering zipper teeth. Leave needle in fabric at top.

If skirt is box-pleated, knife-pleated, or tailored with inverted pleats, stitching along skirt edge must be *under* pleat fold, not on top of it. Starting at bottom edge, stitch zipper to skirt edge under pleat as far up as possible. When you can go no farther, backstitch and raise needle. Move fabric to side so needle is ½ inch in from skirt edge. Tack by taking a few stitches and then backstitching; this tack to the side is to keep zipper and seam allowances from bulging out. Break stitching and begin again at skirtline or just above skirtline welt, making sure you tack before stitching up the length of zipper. Leave needle in fabric at top.

If a slipcover has no skirt, start sewing close to bottom, backstitch, and continue sewing up zipper as you would for a slipcover with skirt. Leave needle in fabric at top.

4 **Stitch across top.** Raise presser foot, turn slipcover 90 degrees, and carefully sew across zipper at top, backstitching to secure zipper ends. Leave needle in fabric.

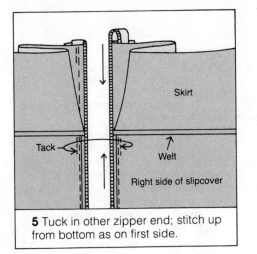

5 Tuck in other zipper end; stitch up from bottom as on first side.

5 Stitch down other side. Raise presser foot, turn slipcover 90 degrees, and sew down other side with a ¼-inch seam (or, if welt occurs on that side, sew along welt, using welt seam as a guide). Make sure pressed edge or welt almost covers zipper teeth.

As you sew, check occasionally to see that ends of welt around bottom of slipcover or at skirtline will meet exactly. If they won't, ease in or gently stretch pressed edge—whichever is required—as you stitch down zipper so ends will match.

If slipcover has a gathered skirt, stop sewing 2 inches from bottom and turn up 1 inch of zipper tape, tucking it between slipcover and seam allowance. Sew to bottom of skirt, backstitch, and break off stitching.

If skirt is box-pleated, knife-pleated, or tailored with inverted pleats, stop stitching and tack when you reach skirtline or skirtline welt. Take slipcover out from under sewing machine needle and turn it around so you can sew the last length of zipper to skirt from the bottom up. To do this, repeat first paragraph of Step 3, "Stitch up zipper." If zipper bulges out a little at skirtline, take a few stitches by hand through zipper tape, seam allowances, and slipcover on both edges near skirtline.

If slipcover has no skirt, sew to bottom edge, backstitch, and break off stitching.

SECURING THE SLIPCOVER

Here are three ways of anchoring your slipcover to the bottom of your furniture to help keep it snug.

If your cover has a skirt and the original upholstery doesn't (or if the original has a skirt with open corners), sew two 10-inch lengths of ¼-inch-wide twill tape to the skirt seam allowance at each leg, and then tie securely behind. Or make your own ties from 10-inch-long, 1-inch-wide fabric strips, folded and stitched to enclose raw edges.

For a snug fit on a skirtless cover, staple or tack the tacking panels to the underside of the furniture's frame.

Or, for easier removal of a skirtless slipcover, anchor the bottom tacking panels to the frame with 2-inch-long, ¾-inch-wide strips of nylon self-gripping fastener spaced 6 to 10 inches apart. (If furniture has a curved bottom edge, strips should be spaced closer. You may also have

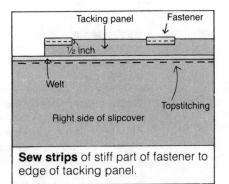

Sew strips of stiff part of fastener to edge of tacking panel.

to fold over and tack down excess fabric so slipcover hugs curved bottom edge.)

Sew a strip of the *stiff* part of the fastener on each tacking panel, with both fastener and panel right side up and fastener overlapping edge of panel by ½ inch. Turn fastener strip toward wrong side of panel and stitch along free edge of fastener.

Place slipcover on furniture, turn furniture upside down, and mark on furniture bottom where matching strips should go. Staple strips of *soft* part of fastener to underside of frame at these positions.

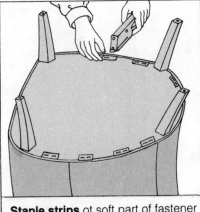

Staple strips of soft part of fastener to frame.

SLIPCOVER PROTECTORS

Arm protectors, headrests—even cushion covers, if you own a rambunctious pet—help keep your slipcover clean and prevent wear.

The simplest slipcover protector is the hemmed rectangle (or oval, if you prefer) draped across the area you wish to protect. When you cut out your protectors, be sure to allow at least an inch all around for hemming. Fasten the protector by inserting twist-pins (available at upholstery supply and fabric shops) at the corners, out of the way of body contact (top boxing or outside back for headrests, outside arms for arm protectors, side boxing for cushions).

A fitted protector requires more work, but is neater-looking and less likely to slip. Arm covers, in particular, are relatively easy to make and serve well to extend the attractive life of your slipcover.

Once you've shaped and sewn a slipcover, you'll find that making fitted arm covers is like traveling familiar territory. Basically, you'll be blocking out, pin-fitting, trimming, and sewing fabric to cover the arms just as you did for the slipcover. The difference is that the lower and back edges of the inside and outside arms, as well as the lower edge of the arm fronts, will extend only the distance you choose and will be finished with double ½-inch hems.

Review the arm construction steps for your slipcover, then proceed:

1. Remove the slipcover but leave cushion in place.

2. Decide on the lower and back limits for your arm covers.

3. To the extent that you want the area covered, block out inside and outside arm as one piece (if you have large enough scraps; if not, seam together), and arm front (if used). Add 1 inch to each edge.

4. Pin-fit as for a slipcover, and trim seam allowances to ½ inch.

5. Sew pinned seams. If you use welt, remember to remove cord from casing in hem area and where seams cross.

6. To hem edges, turn under and press ½ inch all around; turn under and press another ½ inch, then stitch.

Step-by-step: Installing a zipper in a no-welt slipcover

1 **Baste seam.** On a skirted or skirtless slipcover, with right sides together, baste zipper seam allowances together. Be careful not to catch pleat edges of skirt in this basting seam. Press seam allowances open.

2 **Baste zipper to seam allowances.** On wrong side of slipcover, place closed zipper face down over seam allowances, with 1 inch of zipper tapes extending beyond bottom of skirt, or 4 inches beyond bottom of skirtless slipcover. *Sewing through zipper tape and seam allowance only,* start from bottom edge and sew full length of zipper tape on one side, about ¼ inch from zipper teeth. Repeat on other side. Remove seam allowance basting, open zipper, and turn slipcover right side up. Follow Steps 3–5, of "Installing a zipper in a welted slipcover," preceding, disregarding references to welt that do not apply.

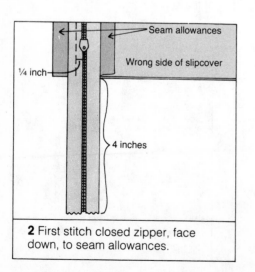

Seam allowances

Wrong side of slipcover

¼ inch

4 inches

2 First stitch closed zipper, face down, to seam allowances.

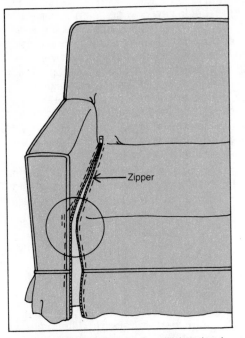

On a sofabed zipper, needle is raised and moved over welt at base of inside arm; stitching resumes on other side.

Installing zippers in a sofabed

A sofabed slipcover requires the usual back zipper. In addition, two front zippers make it possible to unfold the bed without removing the slipcover. Each zipper starts at the bottom and goes up the front arm section (or, on a T-deck, up deck front between main deck and T ear) to the base of the inside arm. Then each zipper turns 90 degrees toward inside arm/deck tuck-in and runs along the base of the inside arm, stopping at the inside back.

When installing front zippers in a sofabed slipcover with welt, follow instructions on pages 94-96 for a welted slipcover. Because front zippers are so visible, it's best not to sew over the front arm welt. Instead, sew up to the base of the inside arm, backstitch, raise the needle and presser foot, move over the welt, backstitch, and then continue sewing up the zipper to the inside back.

Sewing slipcover variations

Even if your furniture doesn't resemble the fully upholstered armchair, read the step-by-step instructions beginning on page 85 for a general idea of how to assemble a slipcover. The way your slipcover is pinned together should suggest an order for sewing its seams; the following paragraphs give some guidelines for the most common variations.

Darts. As a rule, stitch darts first. An exception occurs when you make an unstitched dart to fit a vertical scroll arm without top boxing; in this case, you sew the dart as part of the horizontal inside arm/outside arm seam.

Spring-edge T-deck. A spring-edge crevice, rather than a spring-edge dart, separates deck from arm front on a spring-edge T-deck. Sew spring-edge crevice seam at front (deck and arm front pieces will be basted with a single pin), continuing seam to include inside arm/deck tuck-in, without welt. Later, in one seam, sew outside arm to arm front and side of deck, with or without welt.

Curved deck. If furniture piece has a curved deck, it will have a front boxing piece pin-fitted to deck around curve. Sew top of front boxing to deck, with or without welt; sew side of boxing to arm fronts—or if arms are set back from front, to outside arms—with welt. Leave bottom edge of front boxing free until you are ready to attach skirt or tacking panels.

No top boxing. If slipcover doesn't have top boxing, the top seam joining inside back to outside back should be sewn last, with or without welt. Sewing it last is especially important when you're working on a slipcover for a barrelback chair or a piece of wing furniture.

Barrelback chair. Most barrelback chairs do not have top boxing or shoulders. In these cases, follow this sewing order: Sew vertical seams joining inside back to inside arms and outside back to outside arms, with welt. Then sew horizontal seams joining deck to front boxing (if any) and deck to inside arm/inside back tuck-in, without welt. Finally, join inside of slipcover to outside in one continuous seam, starting at lower front edge and going up over chair to other side, with welt.

Wraparound arms. For a slipcover with wraparound arms, join inside arms to outside arms, where pinned, with welt (there will be no separate front arm sections).

Wings. On wing furniture, outside wings resemble shoulders on the fully upholstered armchair, and inside wings can be thought of as extensions of the inside back. The order for sewing a slipcover for a piece of wing furniture varies somewhat from the sewing order for the fully upholstered armchair. See the drawing of a pin-fitted wing chair for numbered seams that correspond to the following steps.

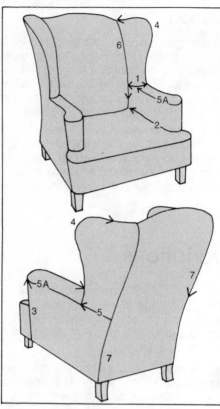

Follow the order of these numbered seams to sew a wing chair slipcover.

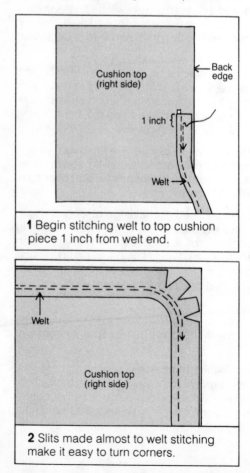

1 Begin stitching welt to top cushion piece 1 inch from welt end.

2 Slits made almost to welt stitching make it easy to turn corners.

After sewing darts, sew inside wing to top or top boxing of inside arm (1), with welt. If deck is a spring-edge T-deck, sew crevice seam at front, continuing seam along inside arm/deck tuck-in to inside back (2), without welt. If deck is curved, sew deck to front boxing, with or without welt. Sew outside arm to arm front and side of deck boxing in one seam (3), with welt. Sew outside wing to inside wing, starting at side and going up across top (4), with welt. Sew outside wing to outside arm (5)—if top boxing, sew outside arm to top boxing, continuing seam all around arm top, ending at base of inside wing (5A), with welt; if no top boxing, continue outside wing/outside arm seam to join outside arm to top of inside arm, ending at unstitched dart, with welt. Sew inside wing to inside back (6), with welt if no tuck-in; if tuck-in, sew welt in seam only from top of chair to where tuck-in begins.

Once seams on front and sides of slipcover are sewn, join outside arm, outside wing, and inside back to outside back, starting seam at outside bottom of slipcover and going up and across top (7), with or without welt.

Cushions

A cushion in good condition can be slipcovered over the original cover. If the cushion you're slipcovering has a form that has begun to deteriorate but still holds its shape, remove the cover and wrap the form with polyester batting; staple or whipstitch the batting around the form. Wrapping the form will soften its edges; should you prefer to build up the top and bottom but keep the edges firm, use spray adhesive to attach cut pieces of batting to top and bottom only.

If the original form is not usable, buy a foam slab and cut pieces to size, using an electric carving knife or serrated bread knife. (Foam is available in different densities and weights. For sources, check the Yellow Pages under "Rubber—Foam & Sponge.") Cover just the foam for a boxed or mock-box cushion; for a soft-box or knife-edge cushion, first wrap the form with batting to soften the edges.

For a knife-edge cushion that's even softer than batting-wrapped foam, make a muslin form and stuff it with a filler such as polyester fiberfill, kapok, foam chips, or down. Cut the muslin pieces the same size as the knife-edge cushion pieces. Stitch the muslin pieces together with a ¼-inch seam, leaving an opening for the filling. Turn inside out, pack firmly, and slipstitch the opening closed.

Step-by-step: Making a boxed cushion

When sewing the slipcover, you slip welt into the seams as you sew them; on the cushions, you'll attach the welt first to the top and bottom pieces and then attach boxing. When sewing welt to cushion piece, stitch along welt seamline; when sewing cushion pieces to boxing, stitch seam between welt seamline and cord.

1 **Stitch welt to top cushion piece.** Beginning and ending at center back edge, lay welt on right side of top cushion piece, welt seam allowance even with raw edges of cushion seam allowance. Begin stitching 1 inch from end of welt.

2 **Turn corners.** Stitch welt to within ½ inch of corner. To turn corner easily, make three diagonal cuts into seam allowance *almost* to welt stitching. Leaving needle in fabric, raise zipper foot, pivot fabric and welt, and continue stitching down other side and around cushion.

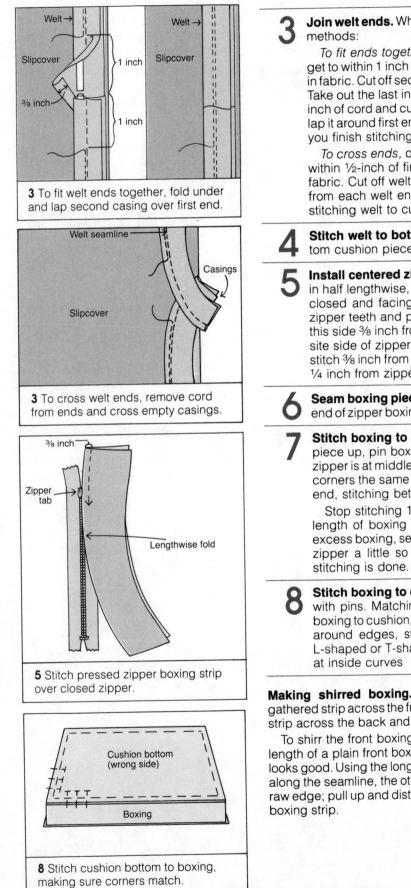

3 To fit welt ends together, fold under and lap second casing over first end.

3 To cross welt ends, remove cord from ends and cross empty casings.

5 Stitch pressed zipper boxing strip over closed zipper.

8 Stitch cushion bottom to boxing, making sure corners match.

3 **Join welt ends.** Where welt ends meet, use either of these finishing methods:

To fit ends together, continue sewing around cushion until you get to within 1 inch of first welt end. Stop stitching, but keep needle in fabric. Cut off second welt end so it will overlap first end by 1 inch. Take out the last inch of casing stitches on second end; pull out 1 inch of cord and cut off. On second end, fold casing under ⅜ inch; lap it around first end. Slip welt back into seam and hold in place as you finish stitching welt to cushion top.

To cross ends, continue sewing around cushion until you get to within ½-inch of first welt end. Stop stitching, but keep needle in fabric. Cut off welt 1 inch beyond needle. Pull out ¾ inch of cord from each welt end and cut off. Cross empty casings and finish stitching welt to cushion top.

4 **Stitch welt to bottom cushion piece.** Repeat Steps 1–3 for bottom cushion piece.

5 **Install centered zipper.** Fold each of the two zipper boxing strips in half lengthwise, right sides out, and press the fold. With zipper closed and facing up, lay one folded edge so it almost covers zipper teeth and pin along tape. Using a zipper foot, stitch down this side ⅜ inch from fold. Lay remaining folded piece over opposite side of zipper so folds meet and cover zipper teeth. Pin and stitch ⅜ inch from folded edge. Baste across ends of zipper tapes ¼ inch from zipper stop and tab.

6 **Seam boxing pieces.** Right sides together, pin and then stitch tab end of zipper boxing to front boxing piece; stitch again for strength.

7 **Stitch boxing to cushion top.** Right sides together and cushion piece up, pin boxing to top cushion piece, making sure center of zipper is at middle of back edge. Zipper ends should come around corners the same distance. Start stitching 1½ inches from boxing end, stitching between welt seamline and cord.

Stop stitching 1½ inches from the first end and determine the length of boxing needed to join with other boxing end. Cut off excess boxing, seam the ends, and finger-press seam open. Open zipper a little so you can turn cushion right side out when all stitching is done.

8 **Stitch boxing to cushion bottom.** Notch boxing corners or mark with pins. Matching these points to bottom cushion corners, pin boxing to cushion, right sides together. With cushion side up, stitch around edges, stitching between welt seamline and cord. On L-shaped or T-shaped cushions, trim seam allowances to ⅜ inch at inside curves

Making shirred boxing. The simplest shirred boxed cushion has a gathered strip across the front and sides and a plain centered zipper boxing strip across the back and around the back corners.

To shirr the front boxing, cut and piece 2½ to 4 times the approximate length of a plain front boxing piece. Experiment to see how much fullness looks good. Using the longest machine stitch, sew two gathering rows—one along the seamline, the other within the seam allowance—along each long raw edge; pull up and distribute fullness. Treat this shirred piece like a plain boxing strip.

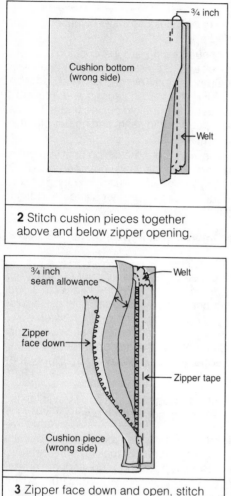

2 Stitch cushion pieces together above and below zipper opening.

3 Zipper face down and open, stitch one side to one seam allowance.

If the back boxing will be exposed, you won't be able to insert a zipper. Shirr enough boxing to go all around the cushion. Stitch the shirred boxing to the top and bottom pieces, leaving most of the back edge open on the bottom piece. Insert cushion or form and slipstitch closed.

Making a knife-edge cushion with welt. Welt, either matching or contrasting, crisply defines the single edge on a knife-edge cushion.

- *Step 1: Stitch welt to top cushion piece.* Follow Steps 1–3 of "Making a boxed cushion," pages 98-99.

- *Step 2: Create the opening for a lapped zipper.* On bottom cushion piece, press under ¾ inch along back edge. (This edge will lap over zipper.) Temporarily fold edge out and, right sides together, pin top and bottom pieces together above and below where zipper will go. Stitch these short seams, backstitching for strength.

- *Step 3: Install lapped zipper.* With right sides of cushion pieces still together and welted piece underneath, pull aside piece that's on top so seam allowance of piece underneath is exposed. Place one side of open zipper face down on seam allowance, zipper teeth on top of welt. Pin and stitch close to teeth from top to bottom of zipper tape, stitching through zipper tape and seam allowance only.

Open out cushion pieces so both right sides are up. (Zipper is now attached on one side, under welt.) Close zipper and lay pressed seam allowance over teeth. Pin and baste on outside. Making sure that stitching catches zipper tape underneath, stitch entire length of back edge, about ⅜ inch from fold. Then open zipper several inches.

- *Step 4: Stitch top and bottom pieces together.* Turn right sides together again and pin other three edges. Keeping welt seamline on top, stitch between welt seamline and cord around cushion. Clip corners diagonally and turn cushion cover right side out. Insert cushion or form and zip closed.

Making a mock-box or soft-box cushion with welt. Like a knife-edge cushion, a mock-box or soft-box cushion has one seam joining top and bottom pieces—it's the corners that give each cushion the look of a boxed cushion.

- *Step 1: Fold in and stitch corners.* Working with top and bottom pieces separately, measure in from each corner half the desired depth of cushion, plus seam allowance (either ½ or ¾ inch, depending on placement of zipper). Make small clips to mark, fold right sides together so clips meet, and stitch a seam from cut edges up to fold. Fold in all corners of top and bottom pieces; stitch. Trim off corner pieces to ½ inch; finger-press seam open.

Another variation, the soft-box corner cushion, is measured and cut out like a mock-box cushion. Instead of stitching corners down, place one pin in each corner perpendicular to cut edges; fold out triangular piece in half so point is centered and extends beyond pin. Baste this fold in place around the corner.

- *Step 2: Complete the cushion.* To attach welt to top cushion piece, see Steps 1–3 of "Making a boxed cushion," pages 98–99. See Steps 2–4 of "Making a knife-edge cushion," above, to install a lapped zipper and stitch top and bottom pieces together.

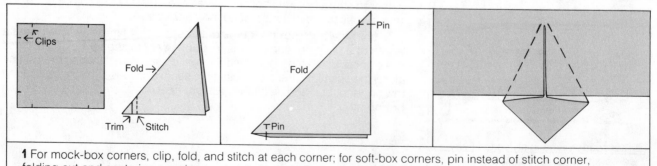

1 For mock-box corners, clip, fold, and stitch at each corner; for soft-box corners, pin instead of stitch corner, folding out and centering ear piece.

BEDSPREADS

How to make throws, quilts, comforters, fitted spreads, skirts & dust ruffles

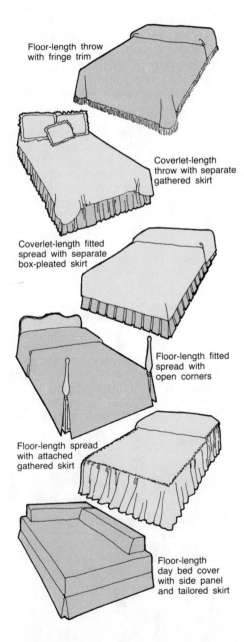

Floor-length throw with fringe trim

Coverlet-length throw with separate gathered skirt

Coverlet-length fitted spread with separate box-pleated skirt

Floor-length fitted spread with open corners

Floor-length spread with attached gathered skirt

Floor-length day bed cover with side panel and tailored skirt

Bedspreads come in styles to fit any bedroom setting. This chapter tells how to make these spreads and others.

Treat the bed to new fabric, and most bedrooms immediately wake up. Just consider the sweeping expanse of even a small day bed—and, in your mind's eye, you'll see the impact possible with new color, fresh patterns, or a change of texture. At the same time, you might give thought to adding a few new touches for extra luxury . . . plump bolsters (explained on page 115), for example, or dainty pillow shams (page 106).

A bedspread can be made of the most delicate, filmy lace or the most rugged, heavy wool, or almost anything in between. It can be one layer thick or a mass of puffy quilting. It can be tailored or frilly, patterned or solid color. It can envelop the whole bed or skim over a dust ruffle.

In this chapter we tell you how to make a throw (a large piece of fabric with minimal seams), a machine-stitched quilt, a tied comforter, a fitted spread (a throw with tailored corners), a spread with attached skirt, and a separate skirt (dust ruffle or petticoat). For each style, we explain how to adapt the technique to suit a day bed (also called studio couch or Hollywood bed).

Sewing Equipment & Fabrics

Constructing a bedspread isn't substantially different from making a slipcover—it's just simpler. Beds don't vary much in style; other furniture varies considerably. You calculate the amount of fabric needed for a spread with measurements, perhaps aided by scale drawings.

Sewing equipment

You'll need a sewing machine, machine needles and hand-sewing needles of the appropriate size for your fabric, color-matched thread, a zipper cording foot if you plan to use welt or shirring tape, pins, an iron and ironing board, bent-shank shears, small scissors, a yardstick, a tape measure, and chalk. Refer to more detailed equipment descriptions and illustrations on pages 34–35 if you have questions concerning this list.

Because you'll be working with lots of fabric, it will be helpful to have a large work surface of convenient height. In a pinch, the floor works fine for laying out material.

Suiting fabric to bedspread style

You are less restricted in your fabric choice for a bedspread than for a slipcover, since spreads usually aren't subjected to as much wear as slipcovers. A possible exception might be day bed covers—these should be made of more durable material. Read the fabric descriptions on pages 36–39 to help you narrow your choice.

If you plan to machine-wash the finished spread, be sure the fabric is preshrunk, or preshrink it yourself before sewing, especially if you plan a fitted spread.

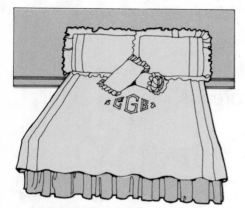

Delicate fabrics are often used for single-layer bedspreads.

A quilt can have a pieced or appliquéd top made of different fabrics.

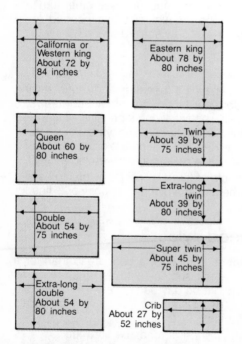

Mattress sizes vary, so measure your bed carefully.

Sheets. If you want to use a light color, especially a solid, or if you have a dog or cat that naps on the bed, consider choosing machine-washable fabric such as bedsheets. Relatively inexpensive, sheets are sometimes used to coordinate a complete room. One of the advantages of sheets is their width: you can often use a single piece of fabric instead of piecing together lengths of 48-inch-wide bolt fabric. On the other hand, you may have to piece sheets to obtain enough length.

Single layer of fabric. With many kinds of fabric, a single thickness can be used for a bedspread, as long as it's not so heavy that its own weight will stretch it out of shape, or so sheer that bedding will show through.

Thin fabrics have traditionally been used as blanket covers under quilts, but blanket covers make very attractive spreads on their own. The most delicate satins and the daintiest cottons can be used; they are often trimmed with lace or ribbon banding.

Quilts and comforters. Closely woven cottons or cotton/polyester blends are probably used most often in quilts, especially in prequilted yardage, but corduroy, velvet, and many other fabrics are also suitable.

Comforters—puffy, coverlet-length quilted throws—are often too bulky to tuck under pillows, but instead call for matching or contrasting pillow shams (page 106) and skirts (pages 113–119) to complete the bed covering.

Sewing techniques for quilts and comforters appear on pages 107–109.

Reversible spreads. Many kinds of fabrics can be used for reversible spreads; the important thing is that they be compatibly paired. They should be reasonably similar in weight so they lie well regardless of which side is up, and their colors, textures, and degree of formality should go well together, since a bit of the underside is almost certain to be visible along the edges. The easiest way to construct a reversible spread is to substitute finish fabric for lining or backing material.

You can even make a separate skirt reversible—just sew a separate lining out of the reverse fabric.

Determining yardage

The size of the bed—*when it is made up with sheets, blankets, and pillows*—is the most important factor in determining yardage. Approximate mattress sizes are shown in the illustration, but it's important to double-check by measuring the particular bed you're planning to cover. Height of the spread (called the "drop") varies, depending on the type of frame used and how much of it you want to cover. With a standard box spring and mattress, the drop from the top edge of the bed to the floor is usually 21 inches, but it varies commonly from 19 to 22½ inches. On platform beds the drop equals the depth of the mattress. If you want the

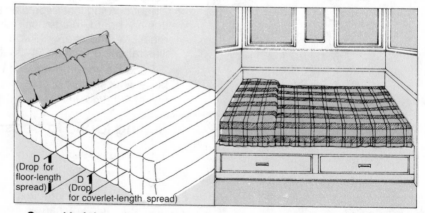

Spread height, or "drop," depends on amount of frame to be covered.

bed frame to show, as you might on some water beds or trundle beds, the bedspread's drop will equal the mattress depth plus a few inches to cover the joint between mattress and frame.

The amount of fabric needed varies according to the style of spread. Specific methods for calculating yardage are included with directions for the different types of spreads. Remember to deduct selvages from the usable width. *In all calculations, be sure to divide total inches by 36 for yards needed.*

Pattern. If the fabric has a large repeat, a vertical (one-way) design, or a stripe or plaid, extra fabric will be needed for centering the design or matching patterns.

Here's how to decide whether or not a fabric needs to be matched: In the store, unroll enough yardage to lay two sections of fabric side by side, selvages aligned and pattern matched so that it continues across the two widths as if they were one. Now shift one section slightly—if the pattern fluctuates jarringly, you should plan to match when you make your bedspread. (If the pattern is printed severely off-grain, don't buy it.)

To determine the additional fabric needed for matching patterns, first measure the repeat height—measure lengthwise from one detail in a motif to the identical detail in the next motif. On some fabrics you'll find the repeat height printed in the selvage.

For each cut piece of fabric that you will sew together to make your bedspread ("cut piece" is the finished piece measurement plus seam and hem allowance), determine the number of repeats you will need. Do this by dividing the cut piece measurement by the repeat height, then rounding off to next higher number. Next multiply the number of repeats needed for each cut piece by the repeat height. This will give you a figure you can use as you determine the yardage for your spread.

Railroading. An economical way to make a bedspread, railroading cuts down on seams as well as on the amount of fabric, and it simplifies matching of patterns. With railroading, the fabric runs the length of the bed (see illustration). Top panels are almost always railroaded on beds; on day beds they are run vertically if there is a one-way design. With both side panels and skirts, to railroad or not to railroad depends on the pattern.

If you're using a patterned fabric to make a spread with a skirt, you may find that you can railroad the bedspread's top panel but not its side panel or skirt. Patterns showing direction (animals, trees, flowers with stems, for example) can look strange turned sideways. Not railroading—running the fabric vertically, instead—increases the number of cut lengths but allows the pattern to run vertically. A print that shows no direction (dots, circles, squares, for example) can be railroaded on both top and side panels. It is best to stay away from vertically running a bedspread's top panel because of the additional seams.

If you're sewing a cover for a day bed that will have one long side against a wall (taking on the look of a couch), you may choose to run the fabric vertically (across the short dimension of the top) instead of railroading it. With bolt fabrics you must seam widths together, but with bedsheets you should be able to make a seamless top panel.

Lining. If you want to line your bedspread, you must determine yardage for this fabric also. Linings are used on bedspreads to add body to thin fabrics or durability to loosely woven ones, to enclose seam allowances, to take the place of a hem (pillowcase-style lining), or to make the spread reversible (see "Reversible spreads," page 102).

Try to select lining material that's the same width as the spread fabric so any seams will fall in the same places. If you can't find such a lining fabric, you might consider cutting the lining from bedsheets. Drapery lining, which comes in 45, 48, and 54-inch widths, is often used to line spreads. The lining should have the same laundering requirements as the spread material. Generally, lining fabric should be lighter weight than the spread fabric (except for reversible spreads), and its color should clearly match or complement the spread.

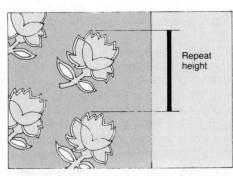

Repeat height in a pattern determines how much extra fabric you'll need.

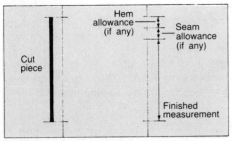

"Cut piece" equals finished measurement plus seam and hem allowances.

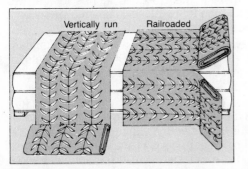

Fabric pattern governs decision to railroad or run vertically.

Basic throw comes down to the floor and has rounded corners.

Keeping It Simple: Throws

A throw is a large rectangular piece of fabric (usually made by seaming three sections together) that extends to the floor or overlaps a separate skirt. If you prefer a more tailored look, you can seam the corners of a throw to make a simple fitted spread. This is most easily done by first constructing a throw, then pin-fitting it to your bed.

Step-by-step: Measuring your bed

Since bed styles and sizes vary surprisingly, you should measure the actual bed made up with the sheets, blankets, and pillows that you'll use with the throw. Keep measurements in inches until you're finished, then convert to yards.

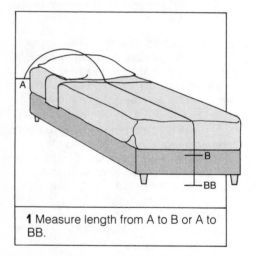

1 Measure length from A to B or A to BB.

1 **Length.** Measure from A (3 inches below top edge of mattress) to B (3 inches past bottom of mattress) or from A to BB (floor) depending on whether you want spread to cover just mattress or reach to floor. If you plan to tuck spread under pillow, add about 17 more inches.

Your mattress may fit snugly against a headboard, and in that case you'll want spread to extend just a few inches beyond pillow instead of all the way to point A on drawing.

Add hem allowance you prefer; it would be 3 inches for the two 1½-inch hems at top and bottom. Or add 1 inch for the two ½-inch seam allowances if you're attaching a pillowcase-style lining (see page 106). Make whatever adjustments are needed to allow you to match motifs in a patterned fabric (see page 103).

If you're using bedsheets and one sheet doesn't have the length you need, you'll have to piece two together; this is difficult to do attractively. A possible solution is to locate the seam at the head of the bed in such a way that it can be tucked under the pillow. Otherwise, we recommend that you choose bolt fabric.

When you're considering sheets for bedspread making, always double-check measurements on the particular sheet design you want to buy. Lengths can vary substantially, as you can see by this sampling: twin (single) and full (double), 96 to 104 inches long; queen, 102 to 106 inches long; king, 102 to 110 inches long. You can gain a few extra inches by removing stitching and using hems.

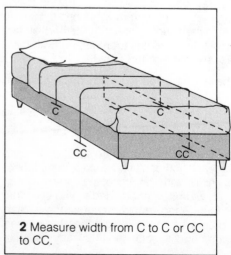

2 Measure width from C to C or CC to CC.

2 **Width.** To arrive at width of spread, measure across bed in several places, from C (3 inches past bottom of mattress) to C, or CC (floor) to CC, depending on whether you want spread to cover just mattress or reach to floor. Width at center of bed may be less; if so, use the lesser measurement. Add 3 inches for the two 1½-inch side hems, or 1 inch for two ½-inch seam allowances if you're using a pillowcase-style lining.

You need to know width of fabric you'll be using. Standard widths of bolt fabrics are 36, 45, 48, and 54 inches. Sheets, of course, are wider: twin size is about 66 inches wide; full, 81; queen, 90; and king, 108.

Divide width of spread (before hemming) by fabric's width (excluding selvages) and round off any fraction to next larger number for the number of widths you'll need. If you need two widths, one whole width will form the center panel and one will be split into two side panels. If you need three, one will form the center panel and a full width will form each side panel. Be sure you have at least 2 inches extra for seams that will join the two side panels to center.

3 **Total.** Multiply length measurement (adjusted for repeat pattern if necessary) by number of widths you need (probably 1, 2, or 3), then divide the result by 36 to convert inches to yards. Don't forget to allow extra fabric if you'll be making welt (see page 85).

Step-by-step: Constructing a throw

Because a throw is by definition loose and unstructured, it is very easy to make. All you do is join fabric widths to make the spread wide enough, then finish the corners and hem the edges (not necessary if you decide on a pillowcase-style lining).

1 **Joining widths.** You may be making a spread out of 48-inch-wide bolt fabric for a twin-size bed with a separate skirt, or you may be using king-size sheets to make a spread for a platform bed. If so, it's possible you'll need only one width of fabric. But in most cases you'll have to join several pieces of fabric to make the spread wide enough. Seams look best if they're a few inches onto the top, not exactly at the edge of the mattress.

Joining widths can be done either decoratively or almost invisibly. If your fabric has a pattern that needs matching, plan the center panel first, then align the side panels to match it.

Should yours be a napped fabric, such as corduroy, brushed denim, or velveteen, be sure the nap on each panel runs from the bed's head to its foot.

Your choice of seams includes welted (see pages 83–86) and plain. You can also use bands of contrasting or complementary trim, either applied on top of a plain seam or actually connecting the panels; keep in mind, though, that wide bands between panels will affect the finished width of your spread, so you'll need to adjust measurements accordingly.

2 **Attached lining.** (See Step 4B for an alternative lining method.) One method of lining is to cut pieces of lining material to duplicate spread pieces, then sew each section—both lining and spread fabric—as if it were one piece of cloth. With this method it is important to finish seam edges so they won't ravel. You'll also have to hem the spread (Step 4A).

3 **Finishing corners.** You can leave the corners square if you like the look of a coverlet's corners coming down to points over the skirt or a floor-length spread's corners bunching on the floor.

If you prefer, you can round the corners (bottom corners for a bedspread, top and bottom for a day bed cover). You can put the spread on the bed wrong side out and pin or chalk where the fabric touches the floor, or you can use the following method:

Fold spread in half lengthwise. Measuring from corner's raw edges, mark intersecting chalk lines at a distance equal to hem (or seam) allowance *plus* drop distance (distance from edge of mattress to hemline). At intersection of the two lines, anchor a pin with a string attached. With string held perpendicular to one of the edges, tie a pencil or chalk where string meets edge. Draw an arc as you would with a compass, then cut off excess fabric.

4a **Hemming.** (If you're making a pillowcase-style lining, follow Step 4B instead.) Finish the hem's raw edge by overcasting by hand, zigzagging, or attaching hem tape. Handstitch for an invisible hem, or machine stitch. You can accentuate the hem by attaching a ruffle, binding the edge with braid, sewing on fringe, or padding the edge with batting. If you use one of these alternate finishes instead of the standard hem, be sure to take into account the

1 With patterned fabric, match side panels to center panel.

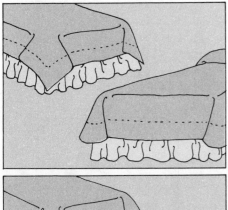

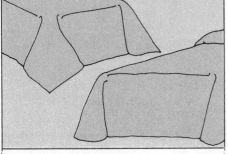

3 Coverlet and floor-length throws can have square or rounded corners.

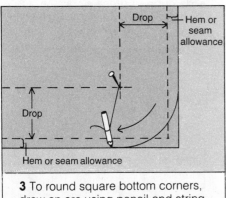

3 To round square bottom corners, draw an arc using pencil and string.

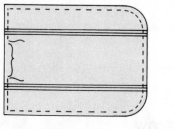

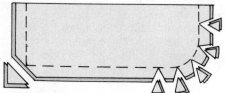

4B Stitch pillowcase-style lining and spread together around edges; clip corners and curves.

inches it may add to the size of your finished throw, and adjust measurements accordingly. If corners have been rounded, you'll need to ease in fullness around corners as you hem.

4b **Pillowcase-style lining.** The simplest way to line a throw is to make a pillowcase-style lining. You simply use fabric that's the same width as spread fabric, sew it as if you were making a duplicate of spread, then attach it to spread.

To attach lining, pin spread and lining with right sides together and stitch around three sides, plus two-thirds of the fourth side (see drawing). Clip seam allowance at curves and corners and finish seam to keep it from raveling, then turn the whole thing right side out. Slipstitch the open portion closed. Tack lining invisibly to the spread along major seamlines.

PILLOW SHAMS

To disguise bed pillows and at the same time dress up a bedroom, consider pillow shams—easy-to-make, knife-edge, loose-fitting pillow covers with simple lapped closures. Here are two styles:

Quick sham. Measure pillow length (long dimension) and width (short dimension) over fullest part. Add 1 inch seam allowance to width; double the length and add 8 inches. Cut fabric piece with pattern running the same direction as bedspread top. Along short edges, turn ¼ inch toward wrong side of fabric; press. Turn under another 1 inch; press and stitch hem.

Center pillow on right side of fabric and mark with pins or chalk along short edges of pillow. Remove pillow and fold fabric along marked lines with right sides together; hemmed edges will overlap.

Pin unhemmed sides, making

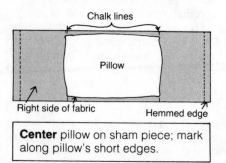

Center pillow on sham piece; mark along pillow's short edges.

sure raw edges are even. Stitch a ½-inch seam along each of these edges (pillow's length). Turn right side out and press. Insert pillow through lapped opening.

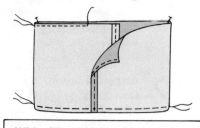

With sides folded in and overlapping, stitch raw edges.

Three-piece sham. Measure pillow length and width over fullest part. Add 1-inch seam allowance to each measurement, and if you want a flange edge (see "Finishes," below), adjust measurements accordingly. Cut one top section to that size.

To make bottom section, cut a piece the same width as top section, but add 5 to 8 inches to length for overlap. Fold fabric in half crosswise and cut on fold.

Now, along each of the edges you just cut from the fold, turn ¼ inch toward wrong side of fabric; press. Turn under another 1 inch; press and stitch hem.

With hemmed edges overlapping at center, pin two bottom sections to top (right sides together). Stitch

bottom to top with a ½-inch seam; clip across corners. Turn sham right side out and press. Insert pillow.

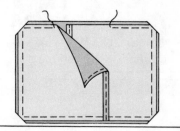

Stitch top piece to bottom sections along raw edges.

Finishes. To a three-piece sham you can add welt (see page 83), or a flange edge.

Make a flange edge by adding desired flange depth (usually 2 to 4 inches) after you've allowed for seams and overlap. Continue as for a three-piece sham. Turn right side out and press. Topstitch 2 to 4 inches (depth of flange) from sham edge.

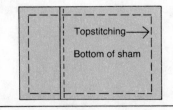

Flange edge gives a tailored finish to pillow sham.

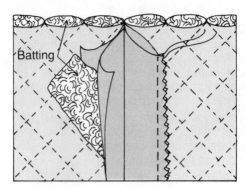

Removing batting from seam allowances reduces bulk.

Quilts & Comforters

Should a quilted bedspread be your goal, you have four choices: you can use prequilted fabric, you can quilt by hand, you can quilt by machine, or you can tie a quilt (also called "tufting").

The first choice, using prequilted fabric, is probably the easiest. You may want to remove the batting from seam allowances (see drawing) to decrease bulk. It would be easier to bind the edges rather than hem them, unless you want the look of a thick hem made by turning under fabric without removing batting.

Quilting by hand is something of an art. See the *Sunset* book *Quilting & Patchwork* for directions.

Step-by-step: Quilting by machine

You can use your sewing machine for quilting, but the process is very time-consuming because hand-basting, rather than pinning, is usually recommended. Still, machine quilting may be just the right look for your bedspread. Here's how to do it.

1 Select batting (sheets of polyester batting, precut to various coverlet sizes, are available in most fabric shops) plus material for top and back of quilt. Allow about 10 percent extra fabric length and width for seams and for the drawing up that occurs as fabric is quilted (allow still more if you use extra-thick batting). If you plan to edge the quilt by bringing backing around over the front, add extra backing fabric equal to width of edging. Press fabric carefully to remove all wrinkles.

2 Make a sandwich: Lay backing material out flat, wrong side up, then position batting on top of it, carefully smoothing from center outward to remove all wrinkles. Cover with quilt top fabric, right side up, again carefully smoothing from center outward.

Beginning at center and working outward, pin all three layers together. Place pins close together all over quilt—about 6 inches maximum distance apart.

3a *Preparing to edge with backing.* If you plan to bring backing material around to edge the front of quilt, you should trim layers to fit now. Trim top layer of quilt so there is a ½-inch seam allowance beyond the point where you want edging to join top layer.

Batting can be a single layer at edge or can be doubled if you want a puffier edge. For a single-thickness edge, batting should extend beyond the edge of quilt's top a distance equal to the finished edging width minus the ½-inch top seam allowance. This will bring batting's edge right to the point where backing folds forward to form a seam allowance. Therefore, backing should extend beyond batting a distance equal to the width of the edging plus ½ inch.

For a double-thickness edge, batting should extend beyond the edge of quilt's top a distance equal to double the edging's width minus the ½-inch top seam allowance. Backing should then extend beyond batting by ½ inch, which will be folded over batting as edge is stitched down.

3b *Preparing to edge with bias strips.* Trim all three layers of quilt—top, batting, and back—evenly to quilt's finished size. As long as there is at least ½ inch of fabric for a seam allowance, the edge of the top can fall short, if necessary, because the outer edge will be covered by bias binding.

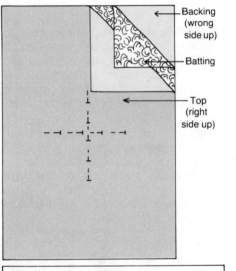

2 Lay batting between backing and top fabric. Pin layers together.

Future seam (where edging joins top layer)

Backing (width of edging plus ½-inch seam allowance)

Exposed batting (width of edging minus ½-inch seam allowance)

Top (½-inch seam allowance)

3A To edge with backing, trim layers to correct sizes.

4 Basting, not just pinning, is usually recommended for machine quilting, because pins pucker the fabric. If you use a contrasting thread color, rows of basting will be easy to see. On the other hand, if you use matching thread, any basting that is difficult to remove (because of being caught up in machine stitching) will not be visible.

Working from center, baste one row along lengthwise grain and one row along crosswise grain. Continuing to work outward from center, baste lengthwise rows and crosswise rows until you have a crosshatching of basting rows covering quilt.

Distance between rows of basting will vary, depending on your fabric and batting. Six inches between rows is a good average, but with slippery fabric and thick batting, you should probably baste rows closer together—as close as every 2 inches. With smooth cotton fabric and thin batting, you could try basting rows as far apart as 12 inches. Baste and stitch a sample to see what will work with your materials.

5a *Stitching straight lines.* Use a sample "sandwich" of your fabrics and batting to check stitch length and tension. You may need to adjust feed dog so quilt will move smoothly under presser foot. A quilting guide—a bar that attaches to the sewing machine and acts as a distance measure when you're stitching parallel seamlines—is a valuable tool. You can buy one to fit your machine at a shop that carries sewing machine parts. For some machines, a special presser foot is available for quilting.

Mark the first vertical and first horizontal lines of quilting with yardstick and chalk or soft pencil, making sure each is straight. Use quilting guide as you sew to make subsequent lines parallel to the first. Roll quilt tightly to make it easier to handle. With sufficient basting, it's not necessary to begin stitching at the center or to alternate vertical and horizontal rows. Remove basting when quilting is finished.

5b *Stitching around motifs.* Use a sample of your quilt to practice on. You may need to lower feed dog so quilt will move smoothly under presser foot. Stitch slowly and carefully, pivoting if necessary. Additional basting helps ensure good results. Remove basting when quilting is finished.

6a *Edging with backing.* Press raw edge of backing to form a ½-inch turnunder (wrong sides together). Bring backing around so it overlaps raw edge of quilt's top by ½ inch. Stitch in place, mitering corners if you wish.

6b *Edging with bias binding.* If necessary, stitch bias binding strips (page 84) together for required length. Then press under ½ inch along edge that will fold toward front. With right side of binding against right side of backing, raw edges aligned, stitch bias binding strips along edges of quilt. Bring binding over quilt top, overlapping top by at least ½ inch, and stitch in place.

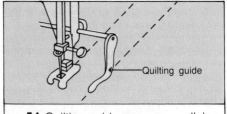

Quilting guide

5A Quilting guide ensures parallel lines of stitching.

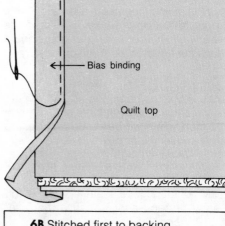

Bias binding

Quilt top

6B Stitched first to backing, bias binding overlaps quilt's top.

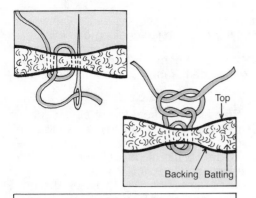

2 Double knot holds together layers on tied or tufted quilt.

Step-by-step: Tying or tufting a quilt

Making a tied or tufted quilt is the fastest way to a custom-made quilted spread or comforter. With tying, you can use the puffiest batting without having to worry about whether your sewing machine can handle it, especially if you edge or hem by hand.

1 Follow Steps 1–3 under "Quilting by machine," page 107.

2 Use pearl cotton or yarn for tying; make certain ties are washable if quilt fabric is washable. Beginning at center of quilt, sew through all three layers twice, then tie a double knot (see drawings). Let fabric motif determine position of ties, or tie in a geometric pattern, but space ties not more than 6 inches apart. Tie ends may appear on top or bottom of quilt; ends should be clipped not shorter than ¾ inch, or may be left as long as you like.

The Easiest Fitted Spreads

The only difference between this style of bedspread and the throw described on pages 104–106 is the corner finish—the fitted corners give a more tailored effect. If you're making a bedspread, you'll fit the two corners at the foot of the bed; for a day bed cover, you'll fit all four corners.

You can choose from three kinds of corner finishes: plain (with sides sewn together), inverted pleats, or open (to fit around bedposts). With any of these, use an attached lining (page 105, Step 2) rather than pillowcase-style lining if you wish to line the spread.

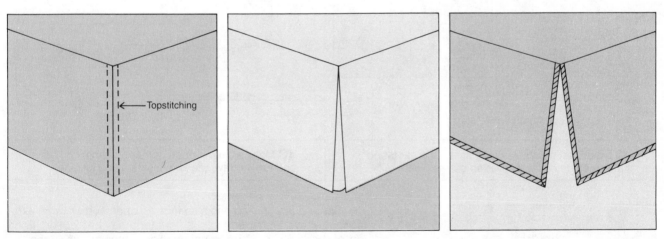

Choose a corner finish—plain, inverted pleat, or open—that suits both spread style and bed.

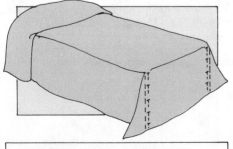

2 To fit corners, pin straight lines following shape of bed.

Step-by-step: Making a fitted spread

1 First follow instructions under "Measuring your bed," pages 104–105, and Step 1 under "Constructing a throw," page 105. If you're lining your spread, follow Step 2 as well.

2 Lay bedspread wrong side up over the bed, which should be made up with pillows and blankets. Arrange spread so it hangs evenly on all sides. Then, starting at the top of a foot corner, pin spread fabric together in a vertical seam that follows the shape of mattress and box spring corners. Don't pull too tightly, and try to pin in a straight line. Do this for both foot corners of a bedspread, for all four corners of a day bed cover. Then take spread off bed.

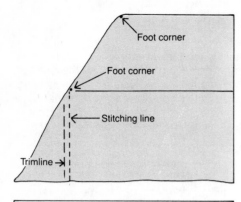

4A Sew corner seams, trim "dart" fabric, and finish raw edges.

3 Mark pin line with chalk, remove pins, and secure the line with a few pins placed horizontally; baste together along chalk line.

4a *Plain fitted corners.* Sew each corner seam, reinforcing by stitching twice. Trim excess "dart" fabric ½ inch from stitching line. Finish raw edges.

4b *Inverted corner pleats.* Crease a fold from top of corner "dart" fabric to tip; iron, pin, or mark this foldline. Spread open and flatten "dart" in corner fabric so foldline runs directly along basted line and there is a fold on each side of it. Trim off point of fabric even with bottom edge. Press side folds and topstitch 1/16 inch from edge. Turn spread right side out and remove basting. Leave pleat edges plain, or, for a finished look, topstitch or bind edges with braid.

4c *Open corners.* These are almost essential if you want to fit a spread around bedposts or a footboard. There are two ways to finish open corners. For either finish, begin by marking a parallel cut line 1 inch outside the line you marked in Step 3; cut.

  • *First option:* One inch down from top of corner, mark a dot on the Step 3 foldline. Stitch from dot to top of corner. Remove any basting from foldline and turn raw edges to inside along foldline. Finish raw edges; press. Topstitch or bind open edges for a finished look.

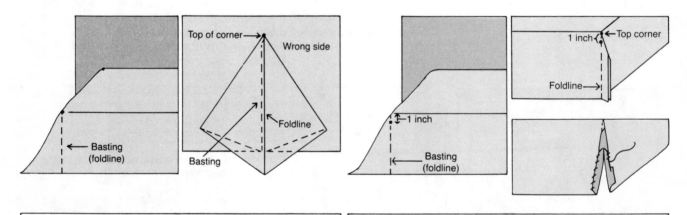

4B Deep dart made on wrong side of corner fabric flattens out to become inverted corner pleat.

4C Make a simple open corner by trimming dart and turning raw edges to inside along foldline.

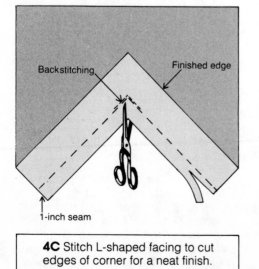

4C Stitch L-shaped facing to cut edges of corner for a neat finish.

  • *Second option:* You can also face an open corner. From extra fabric, cut two L-shaped facings (four for a day bed cover). Each leg of the "L" should be 3 inches wide. Inner edges of the "L" should each be as long as the line you just cut along spread's corner. Finish outer raw edges of facings, then pin facings to spread, right sides together. Stitch 1 inch from edge, reinforcing point with backstitching. Trim seam to ⅜ inch and clip to—but not through—backstitching at point. Turn facing to inside and press; handstitch in place if you wish.

5 Hem spread (Step 4A under "Constructing a throw," page 105).

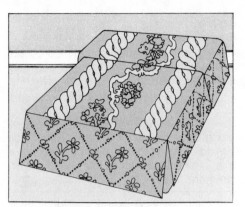

Coordinated fabrics on spread top and skirt give mix-and-match look.

Spreads with Attached Skirts

This type of spread has a panel covering the top of the bed, and a skirt attached at the sides and foot (with a day bed, also at the head). The attached skirt can reach to the floor, or it can cover just the mattress (coverlet length). It can take several forms: straight with inverted pleats at corners; knife or box pleated all around; or gathered. Some skirts are attached directly to the top panel; others start low on the sides of the spread, with a side panel between the top panel and the skirt.

The skirt fabric should be one that drapes well. It can be different from the fabric used for the top panel. Yardage requirements for the top panel, skirt, and possible side panels are outlined separately. If your spread will be made entirely of one fabric, add the yardage figures together. Remember that when you measure, the bed should be made up with the sheets, blankets, and pillows you'll be using with the spread.

Step-by-step: Making the top panel

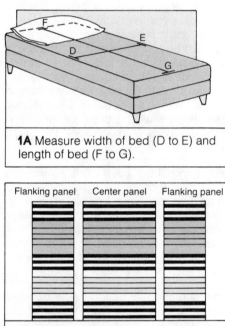

1A Measure width of bed (D to E) and length of bed (F to G).

1a *Railroaded.* Measure width of bed (D to E) and add 1 inch (for the two ½-inch seams to attach skirt or side panel). Divide this figure by fabric's width and round off any fraction to next larger number. If resulting number is two, you'll have to attach two flanking panels to the center panel, so you'll need 2 more inches for seam allowances. If resulting number is three, you'll need four panels—and 3 extra inches will be required for seam allowances.

1b *Vertically run.* If you're making a day bed cover and want fabric on top panel to run across short dimension of bed, follow Step 1A, measuring *length* of bed (F to G) instead of width. You may prefer to join fabric with one seam at center of top panel rather than use one wide panel and two flanking panels; if so, add 1 inch instead of 2 for a seam. If your fabric is narrow or if you don't want a seam at center, add an additional 1 inch for each seam. Adjust as needed for matching motifs (see page 103).

Flanking panel	Center panel	Flanking panel

4 Align stripes when stitching flanking panels to center panel.

2a *Railroaded.* Measure length of top surface of bed (F to G), adding 17 inches for a tuck-in allowance under pillow, if you wish. Add 1 inch for the two seam allowances on a day bed cover; add 2 inches for one seam allowance (½ inch) plus a top hem (1½ inches) if you're making a bedspread.

2b *Vertically run.* For a day bed cover that isn't railroaded, measure *width* of bed (D to E). Add 1 inch for seam allowances. Adjust as needed for matching motifs (see page 103).

3 Multiply final figure from Step 2, A or B, by the rounded number you reached by division in Step 1, A or B. This is total yardage needed for top panel.

4 If necessary, sew together center panel and flanking panels (or sew center seam for top of a day bed cover), matching any large motifs, plaids, or stripes. Use any style seam you want; add welt if you wish (see pages 83–86).

5 For a perfect fit, you'll want your corners to duplicate the mattress shape. Place heavy paper or cardboard between mattress and box spring and trace shape of corner onto paper. Cut out shape and use it as a pattern for fitted corners, being sure to leave a ½-inch seam allowance.

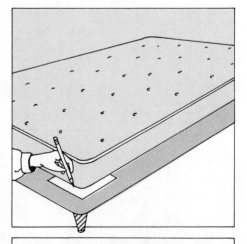

5 Duplicate mattress corner shape by making pattern for top panel corners.

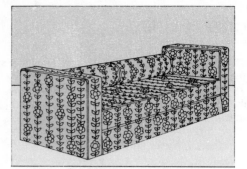

Vertical design requires vertically run side panel.

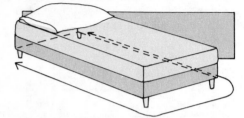

1 Measure around three sides of bed, four sides of day bed.

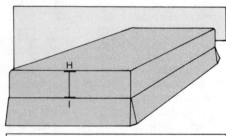

2 Measure finished panel height. (H to I).

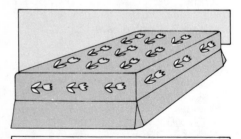

3A Railroaded side panel.

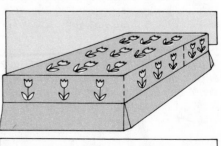

3B Vertically run side panel.

Step-by-step: Making an optional side panel

In this style of bedspread, a panel of fabric—sometimes called "boxing"—runs along the side of the bed, forming a link between the top and the skirt. The skirt attached to it can be any style.

If the fabric has a vertical design, you may prefer not to railroad the side panel.

1 Measure around bed—along three sides for a bedspread, four sides for a day bed cover. Add 3 inches for head-of-bed hem for a bedspread, or 1 inch for a joining seam for a four-sided cover. This is your length measurement.

2 Measure finished height of panel (H to I), being sure point I will fall a few inches below base of mattress; add 1 inch for seam allowances. Add extra inches if needed for centering or matching motifs (page 103).

3a *Railroaded.* Divide width of your fabric by final panel height figure (from Step 2). If result is a number between 1 and 2, the amount of fabric you need to buy equals length measurement (Step 1). For example, if your panel height will be 25 inches and fabric width is 45 inches, divide 45 by 25. The number, 1.8, is between 1 and 2; therefore you'll need an amount of fabric equal to the length measurement. If it's between 2 and 3, buy half the length measurement plus 1 inch for a seam; if it's between 3 and 4, buy one-third the length measurement plus 2 inches for seams. If necessary, cut fabric lengthwise (parallel to selvage) and seam pieces together to achieve required length.

3b *Vertically run.* First subtract 1 inch from your fabric's width (to allow for seams joining sections); then divide distance around bed (Step 1) by fabric's width. Divide the number you reached in Step 1 by this reduced fabric width; this gives you the number of widths you need. Multiply number of widths by adjusted height of panel (Step 2), for inches of fabric you'll need. Cut fabric into number of widths you need (each cut length should measure the adjusted height of panel) and stitch vertical edges together.

4 With right sides together, pin and/or baste optional side panel to top panel, using ½-inch seam allowances. Then stitch—of the many types of seams possible, plain, topstitched, flat-fell, and welted seams (pages 83–86) are most popular.

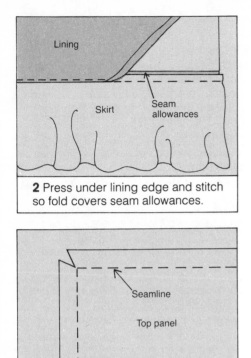

2 Press under lining edge and stitch so fold covers seam allowances.

3 Make V-shaped cut at each top panel corner before stitching to skirt.

Step-by-step: Completing the spread

1 Make a skirt, following directions that begin below. Instead of attaching skirt to a deck or to the bed, refer to the following steps.

2 *Optional lining.* Using lining fabric, make a lining for top panel (or for top panel plus side panel) by following preceding directions for panels. Linings are easiest to make if lining fabric is the same width as spread material and has the same laundering requirements.

Tack lining to spread, wrong sides together, along seam lines.

If spread fabric is fairly lightweight, follow Step 3 to stitch skirt to panels, catching lining in seam along with panel fabric.

If fabric is thick or if you want a more finished look, pin skirt to panels, right sides together, and stitch, following Step 3 but without catching panel lining (be sure lining as well as panel fabric has a V-shaped cut at each corner, as described in Step 3). Press seam toward panels. Fold raw edge of panel lining under ½ inch and pin so fold just covers seam joining skirt to panels. Attach lining by hand, or machine stitch along same stitching line used to join skirt to panels.

3 Pin skirt to top panel or to optional side panel, right sides together. Make a V-shaped cut within seam allowance at each top panel corner (see drawing). It is worthwhile to first baste the skirt on, then fit spread onto bed to make sure it hangs correctly. Stitch skirt to spread, choosing type of seam that is appropriate for weight of fabric and style of skirt.

Skirts & Dust Ruffles

These finishing touches may be joined to the top or side panel of a spread, or they may be sewn separately to a piece of fabric, called the "deck," that slides between the box spring and the mattress. In some cases, the skirt can be hung from rods attached to bedposts.

If, because of a nap or a vertical pattern, your fabric cannot be railroaded, you'll have to do quite a bit more seaming as you construct the skirt. Be sure to follow the steps marked "vertically run" that follow.

A skirt can be self-lined, lined with a different fabric, or simply hemmed. Self-lining is done either by folding a wide piece of fabric in half lengthwise or by stitching together two lengths of a narrower fabric (for the latter, follow the directions for "Skirt with separate lining," page 114). Lining with a separate fabric is done by stitching the lining to the length of skirt material at the lower edge; you'll need the same amount of lining fabric as skirt material if the skirt fabric is railroaded. If it's vertically run, you'll need less lining material, because the lining will be railroaded even though the face fabric isn't. Both self-lining and lining with a different fabric provide an invisible bottom finish. If you're planning a pleated or gathered skirt and want to hold down the quantity of lining material, you can make a completely separate lining, following directions for a tailored skirt (page 116).

Step-by-step: Beginning the skirt

1 Measure around bed—along three sides for a bedspread, four sides for a day bed cover.

2 If skirt will be gathered, multiply distance around bed by 2, 3, or 4, depending on fullness you want and on weight of fabric: for firm fabrics, use two times the distance around bed; for light to medium-weight fabrics, three times; for sheers or semisheers,

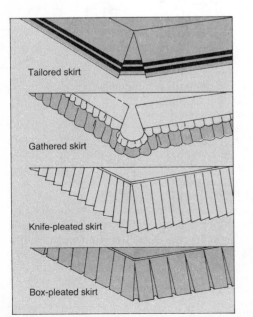

Tailored skirt

Gathered skirt

Knife-pleated skirt

Box-pleated skirt

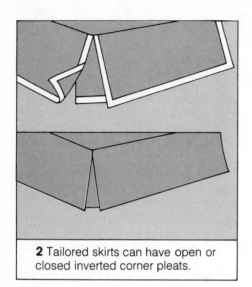

2 Tailored skirts can have open or closed inverted corner pleats.

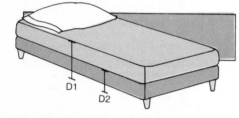

4 Measure finished skirt height (D1 or D2).

Finished skirt height plus hem or lining allowance

7A For railroaded skirt, cut strips parallel to selvage.

four times. Heavy fabrics usually do not gather nicely; instead, consider unpressed box pleats for a soft effect.

You will be dealing with the two foot corners for a bed, with all four corners for a day bed. For a tailored skirt with closed inverted corner pleats, add 24 inches for each corner to distance around bed. For open inverted corner pleats on a tailored skirt, add 12 inches per corner. If you plan a skirt with knife pleats or box pleats, multiply distance around bed by 3¾.

To open up corners to accommodate bedposts or a footboard, add 1 additional inch for each open corner, for seam allowances. Open corners are suitable for any style skirt.

Make any adjustments necessary for centering or matching motifs (see page 103).

3a *Railroaded.* Add 3 inches for the two 1½-inch head-of-bed hems on a spread with a skirt around three sides of bed; or add 1 inch for a joining seam if skirt goes around all four sides of a day bed.

3b *Vertically run.* Subtract 1 inch from fabric's width (excluding selvages) to allow for seams joining sections. Divide the number you reached in Step 2 by this reduced fabric width.

You'll need 3 inches for the two 1½-inch head-of-bed hems. So, if your division came out to a whole number or had a remainder of less than 3, round off to next larger number. This is the total number of fabric widths you'll need.

4 Determine finished height of skirt. Add ½ inch for top seam allowance. Add more for an exposed heading or for a casing for gathering the skirt onto rods (see page 119). Make any adjustments necessary for centering or matching motifs (see page 103); motifs are usually centered vertically on the finished skirt if it is attached to spread, or on the lower third if it is separate.

5a *Self-lined skirt.* Double the number reached in Step 4.

5b *Skirt with separate lining.* Add ½ inch for seam allowance to the number reached in Step 4.

5c *Hemmed skirt.* Add 1½ inches for hem allowance to the number reached in Step 4.

6a *Railroaded.* Divide your fabric's width (excluding selvages) by your result from Step 5 (A, B, or C). If the number you reach is 1 to 2, buy fabric equal to your skirt length measurement (Step 3A). If the number is 2 to 3, buy half your length measurement. If it's 3 or more, buy one-third your length measurement.

6b *Vertically run.* Take the number you reached in Step 5 (A, B, or C) and multiply it by the number of fabric widths you need (Step 3B). Result is amount of fabric you need to buy.

7a *Railroaded.* Cut, parallel to selvage, a long strip of fabric. Width of strip should equal finished skirt height plus hemming or lining allowance (Step 5). If there is a motif, cut each section so motif will be on lower third of finished skirt (it will be visible if a separate spread covers upper skirt area). If skirt will be attached to a spread, you may prefer to center motif vertically. Strip of fabric should go around bed with allowance for pleats or ruffles if desired (Step 3A). If in Step 6A you found that your fabric had a more-than-adequate width, you must cut and seam together two or more long strips of fabric to form the one strip.

BOLSTERS

Behold the bolster—a decorative, structured pillow to use on a chair, sofa, day bed, or bed. Let it repeat or complement your room's colors and textures.

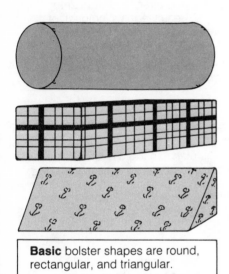

Basic bolster shapes are round, rectangular, and triangular.

Unless you're covering a bolster you already have, buy a precut form from a foam dealer. Or, for a soft, round bolster, sew and stuff a muslin form; use the directions that follow, but slipstitch the opening after stuffing.

As you plan your cover, consider the direction of the fabric on the furniture where the bolster will rest. To add welt, see page 83.

For all bolsters, first determine the form's dimensions (center section plus end pieces). Add ½ inch to each edge; if you plan to install a zipper, add ¾ inch to the edges where the zipper will go.

Round bolster. Cut center section and two circular ends. If you plan to slipstitch the opening, leave a lengthwise opening 3 inches shorter than finished bolster length.

For a zippered closure, buy a heavy-duty zipper (available at upholstery supply stores and some fabric stores) that's 3 inches shorter than finished bolster length. At some stores you can buy a zipper by the inch from a continuous roll.

Right side of fabric up, pin closed zipper face down along one lengthwise edge; place teeth ¾ inch in from cut edge. Using zipper foot, stitch through zipper tape and seam allowance close to teeth. Backstitch at beginning and end.

Turn zipper so right side faces up, zipper tape and seam allowance folded away from zipper. On right side, stitch through all thicknesses close to zipper teeth.

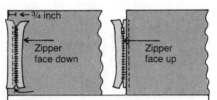

First stitch zipper face down along edge; then turn face up and stitch through all thicknesses.

Fold under and press a ¾-inch seam allowance on other lengthwise edge. Open zipper; lay folded seam allowance over teeth. On right side, stitch ⅜ inch from edge for length of zipper. Backstitch at beginning and end. Close zipper.

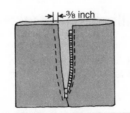

Stitch folded seam allowance to other side of zipper.

Above and below zipper, pin edges right sides together and stitch a ¾-inch seam. Open zipper.

Pin end pieces to center section, right sides together; stitch. Clip into seam allowances of round end pieces at intervals. Turn right side out, press, and insert form. If you didn't install a zipper, slipstitch opening closed.

Square bolster. Cut center section and two square end pieces. Refer to round bolster directions for center section seam and zipper installation. Along end edges of center section pieces, measure and mark points where corners will occur.

When sewing end pieces to center section, have center section on top, end piece below. Stitch along one side to within ½ inch of corner edge; raise presser foot with needle still in fabric. Clip into seam allowance of center section toward, but stopping short of, needle. Pivot fabric on needle one-quarter turn and sew next side. Repeat for all sides. Turn right side out, press, and fill. Slipstitch opening if you didn't install a zipper.

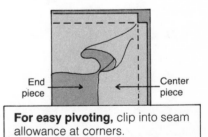

For easy pivoting, clip into seam allowance at corners.

Triangular bolster. You can cut cover either in three sections (one center and two end pieces) or five sections (three center and two end pieces). Seam center pieces to make center section, leaving one edge for zipper or slipstitched closure. Follow construction directions for the square bolster.

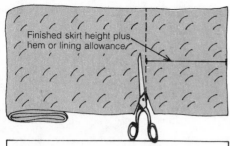

7B For vertically run skirt, cut strips perpendicular to selvage.

7b *Vertically run.* Cut several lengths of fabric perpendicular to selvage, each equal to finished skirt height plus lining or hem allowance (Step 5). If there is a motif, cut each section so motif will be on lower third of finished skirt (it will be visible if a separate spread covers upper skirt area). If skirt will be attached to a spread, you may prefer to center motif vertically. Seam sections together at selvages, using ½-inch seam allowances, to form a continuous strip of fabric that will reach around bed with enough extra for pleating or ruffling if desired (Step 2).

8a *Self-lined skirt.* Fold fabric in half lengthwise, wrong sides together. Tack together at top.

8b *Skirt with separate lining.* Follow directions for determining yardage for a railroaded skirt. Result equals amount of lining material to buy. Then complete Step 7A, using lining fabric.

Sew lining to bottom of skirt, right sides together, using a ½-inch seam allowance. Turn so wrong sides are together, press, and pin top of skirt to top of lining.

8c *Hemmed skirt.* Turn up a 1½-inch hem at bottom of skirt and stitch in place.

9 Finish top edge of skirt strip. If skirt has open corners or open inverted corner pleats, or if you plan to hang a gathered skirt from rods, you must finish corners or ends before finishing top edge.

Follow directions for completing the skirt style you've chosen.

Skirts with open corners

To make a skirt with open corners to accommodate bedposts or a footboard, you will first need to measure for and construct the strip of skirt fabric described in Steps 1–7, preceding. At that point, you should cut the strip into three sections (or four for a day bed), one for each side or end of the bed. Figuring how long each section should be is easy for a tailored skirt without corner pleats—just measure the bed's side or end and add seam or hem allowances. For a gathered or pleated skirt, you must allow for fullness (Step 2, preceding) for each section.

After you've cut the strip into sections, you'll need to finish the ends of each section. For a lined skirt, follow Step 8A or 8B, with this exception: Before you pin the top of the skirt to the lining, turn the section inside out, so right sides are together, and sew a ½-inch seam across each end. Then turn right side out and complete. For an unlined skirt, hem each end by turning under the ½-inch seam allowance; for a more finished look, you may wish to use seam tape.

To attach the skirt sections to a panel or fitted sheet, follow the same steps as for any skirt, but ignore instructions to sew ends together.

Tailored skirts with various corner finishes

Tailored skirts with *closed* inverted corner pleats have a look that is often seen on slipcovers. *Open* inverted corner pleats fall fluidly over the rounded edges of some beds and have underlay flaps.

Step-by-step: Closed inverted corner pleats

1 With skirt right side out, make two inner folds, each 6 inches deep, at each bed corner on your strip of skirt fabric. Make sure edges of folds meet exactly at corner. Baste all layers of fabric together along top. On a day bed, start the skirt strip (where the seam will go) at the least visible corner.

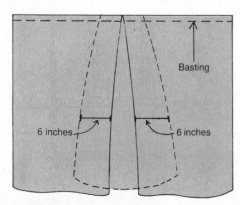

Closed inverted corner pleats are the most tailored.

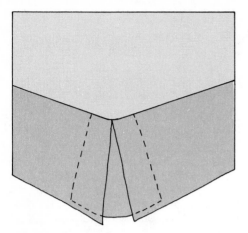

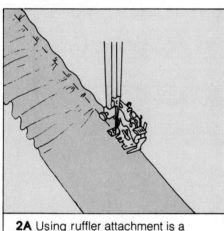

Underlay flap gives smooth look to open inverted corner pleats.

Step-by-step: Open inverted corner pleats

1 For each corner, cut an 11-inch section of fabric from strip of skirt material. These sections will be corner underlay flaps.

2 Finish raw edges of underlay flaps. If skirt is lined, for each underlay flap turn skirt fabric and lining right sides together, seam the sides (leaving top edge open) and turn flap right side out. If skirt is not lined, you can overcast side edges of underlay flaps or turn each of them under and make a ½-inch hem.

3 Measuring carefully, cut through strip of skirt fabric at each corner. Leave a ½-inch seam allowance at each edge of cut. Finish raw edges of each corner by 1) sewing lining to skirt, right sides together; 2) trimming edges ½ inch and overcasting or applying binding; or 3) making a ½-inch hem on each side.

4 Baste an underlay flap at each corner. Finish top edge of skirt strip.

Step-by-step: Gathered skirts (dust ruffles)

You can gather a skirt by using a sewing machine ruffler attachment, by pulling a thread from rows of gathering stitches, by pulling a piece of sewn-on string, or by using shirring tape.

1a *Seam finish.* Whether you want top edge of skirt to form a heading (remaining outside the seam) or to be enclosed in a seam, you should finish the edge with your choice of seam finish before gathering it (except for casing, Step 1B).

1b *Casing for rod.* Make head-end and corner hems for a bed or corner hems for a day bed. Turn under ¼ inch on raw edge of skirt. Turn under again, a distance equal to a 1-inch heading plus rod casing depth. (Make a small test casing first, to determine proper depth; casing should be snug but not too tight.) Stitch close to first fold; then make a second row of stitching above the first to form casing.

2a *Ruffler attachment.* Starting 1½ inches from end (½ inch for day bed), stitch skirt fabric strip, right side up, ½ inch down from top edge (can be further away if you're making optional heading, but be sure you've allowed enough fabric). Stop 1½ inches short of the other end (½ inch for day bed).

2b *Pulling a thread.* Using 100 percent polyester thread (for strength), sew two rows of gathering stitches, one on seamline and the other ¼ inch within seam allowance. Break up stitching occasionally—it's easier to gather small sections. Gather by pulling bobbin threads, distributing fullness evenly, until skirt is correct length.

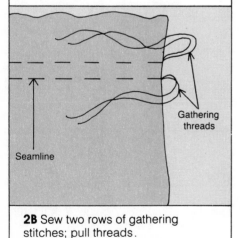

2A Using ruffler attachment is a simple way to gather skirt strip.

Gathering threads

Seamline

2B Sew two rows of gathering stitches; pull threads.

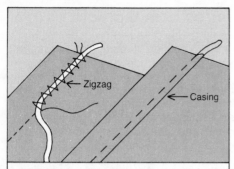

2C String under zigzagging or in casing forms gathers when it's pulled.

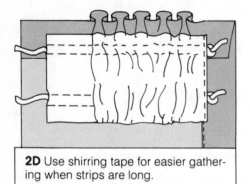

2D Use shirring tape for easier gathering when strips are long.

2c *String.* Lay a length of string inside seamline along top of your length of skirt fabric. Either zigzag over string, being careful not to sew through it, or sew a casing for it using straight stitches. Secure one end of string firmly by stitching across it. Gather by pulling up string, distributing fullness evenly, until skirt is correct length. When gathers are evenly spaced, stitch them in place, running the line of stitching below the string.

2d *Shirring tape.* This flat tape with two cords woven through it makes long sections of fabric easier to gather; it gives double to quadruple fullness. Cut a strip or strips of tape the length of each skirt section plus ½ inch. Turn under ends of tape and pin tape to wrong side of skirt below top seam allowance. Stitch close to both long edges, using a zipper foot to avoid stitching over cords. Knot cords together at one end. Gather by pulling up cords, distributing fullness evenly, until skirt is correct length. Tie cords together at other end to keep them from slipping.

Step-by-step: Knife pleats

1 Starting 1½ inches from one end of skirt fabric strip (½ inch for day bed cover), mark off 1-inch divisions. (This is for 1-inch-wide pleats; your fabric motif may call for a different pleat width.) Mark divisions along entire length of skirt fabric, stopping 1½ inches (½ inch for day bed) short of the other end. Number the marks from 1 to 3, repeating until you reach other end of skirt fabric.

2 Make folds (as shown in drawing) at numbers 2 and 3. Pin in place. Try skirt on bed and adjust width of a few pleats at head end (or at the two less visible corners of a day bed) so a pleat edge, not the middle of a pleat, will fall at each corner.

3 If you want especially sharp pleats, stitch close to the edge along each fold line. Baste pleats in place.

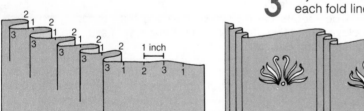
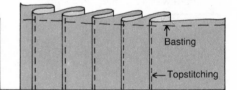

1-3 Measure and number knife pleat divisions, make folds (allowing for any motifs), and baste at top edge. Topstitching is optional for box and knife pleats.

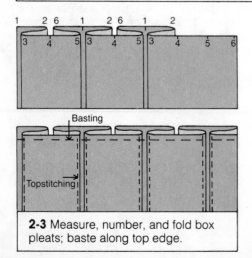

2-3 Measure, number, and fold box pleats; baste along top edge.

Step-by-step: Box pleats

1 Starting 1½ inches (½ inch for day bed cover) from one end of the strip of skirt fabric, mark off 2-inch divisions. (This is for 4-inch-wide box pleats; your fabric motif may demand a different pleat width.) Mark these divisions along entire length of skirt fabric, stopping 1½ inches (½ inch for day bed) short of the other end. Number the marks from 1 to 6, repeating until you reach other end of skirt fabric.

2 Make folds (as shown in drawing) on numbers 2, 3, 5, and 6. Pin in place. Try skirt on bed and adjust width of a few pleats at head end (or at the two less visible corners of a day bed) so that a box pleat edge, not the middle of a pleat, will fall at each corner.

3 If you want especially sharp pleats, stitch close to the edge along fold lines 3 and 5 for each pleat. Baste pleats in place.

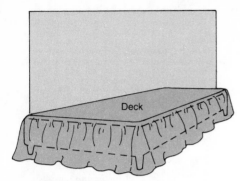

Skirt can be stitched to fabric panel called "deck."

Step-by-step: Attaching skirt to a deck or fitted sheet

A fabric panel—the deck—rests on top of the box spring and is held in place by the weight of the mattress. You can use muslin or any other closely woven material for the deck—polished cotton and drapery lining are also suitable, making a deck that is firm, not flimsy. A color that matches the skirt fabric is best.

1 Determine size of deck by measuring length and width of the top of box spring. Figure exact yardage for deck by following the five steps under "Making the top panel," page 111.

Or attach skirt to a fitted sheet instead of to a deck.

2 Remove mattress and either lay decking material on box spring or place fitted sheet around box spring. Outline upper edge with chalk. Remove from bed.

3a *Deck.* If skirt is for a day bed, first seam ends of skirt together (unless corners will be open). Pin skirt to deck, right sides together if you're making a plain seam. Align corners carefully. Stitch, using a ½-inch seam allowance. Trim seam allowance if necessary.

If skirt is for a bed, hem head end of deck-plus-skirt.

3b *Fitted sheet.* If you're using a fitted sheet for a deck, first hem ends of bedspread skirt or seam together ends of day bed skirt. Pin skirt to sheet, wrong side of skirt against right side of fitted sheet. Stitch, using a ½-inch seam allowance.

4 *Optional heading.* If you're making optional heading on a gathered skirt, attach skirt to edge of deck or fitted sheet with two rows of stitching on right side of skirt; wrong side of skirt will be against right side of deck or sheet.

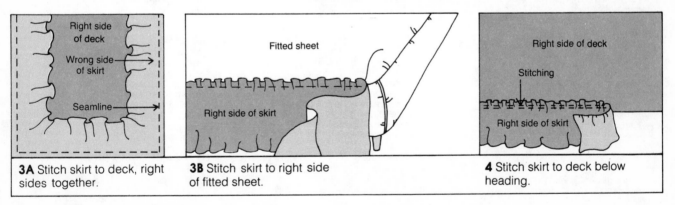

3A Stitch skirt to deck, right sides together.

3B Stitch skirt to right side of fitted sheet.

4 Stitch skirt to deck below heading.

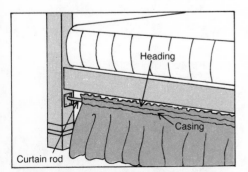

Gathering skirt on rods between bed posts is another option.

Step-by-step: Skirt attached directly to bed

On beds with heavy posts at the corners, you can hang the skirt from ⅜-inch brass-finish café curtain rods. The right rod is important—because of the length involved, sagging could be a problem.

1 Hem ends of skirt.

2 Measure between posts to determine length of each rod. Install rods below the side boards and footboard (headboard too on a day bed). Insert rod through casing and attach to bed frame.

Index